INVISIBLE MONSTER

BY SARAH HAYES

INVISIBLE MONSTER By **Sarah Hayes**

DISCLAIMER: This is a work of creative nonfiction. The events are portrayed to the best of Sarah Hayes's memory. Some stories, names and identifying details, as well as locations have been changed to protect the privacy of the people involved.

ISBN 978-1-7368464-0-7

First Edition
Printed in the United States of America

Dedicated to my husband, Scott, whose constant love and support has given me the strength and confidence to be who I am today, and today I have a beautiful life. You are my forever!

"Suddenly she felt strong and happy. She was not afraid of the darkness or the fog and she knew with singing in her heart that she would never fear them again. No matter what mists might curl around her in the future, she knew her refuge."

Gone with the Wind

Part I

Kolasi, West Virginia 1994

He asked me if I remembered what we used to do in the woods. I remembered, but I was quick to say that I didn't.

1 ~ Tal, Ohio

My birth story is rather amazing! I was born on November 22nd, 1978, in a log cabin with no electricity or running water. I was delivered by my father, with the guidance of a midwife. My birth story is nowhere close to typical, which seems to have paved the way for everything else in my non-typical life.

I feel an introduction of my parents with a little background information will make my birth story make a little more sense. My parents are both from Ohio, my father from Xenia, my mother from Kettering. They both came from loving, "normal" homes with good parents and stability. They met through common friends and fell in love. They decided to "be free", as did most young people of their time. My parents hitchhiked across the country multiple times and settled wherever they landed. They were in Texas for a while, and then Idaho, where they lived on a homestead farm with a group of young people. They grew their own food and lived 100% off their land.

When my mother became pregnant with my brother my parents decided to move back to Ohio and get married. They eventually landed in southern Ohio in a small town called Tal where they merged right in with a small community of fellow "hippies." The men, my dad included, would build log cabins for these families to live in. One of these log cabins ended up being my place of birth, as well as my younger sister, Scarlett's place of birth.

As it turned out, my mother and her friend from one of the log cabin families got pregnant at the same time. My mother and her friend were side-by-side through their entire pregnancies. I feel I should add, my mother had a horrible experience delivering my brother, Gerald, in a hospital, so I was to be born at home with a midwife. On the evening of November 22nd, 1978, my mother went into labor with me. My parents went to find the midwife since I was going to be born soon, but she was already tied up. My mother's friend had also gone into labor at the exact same time, so my parents went to the friend's log cabin.

My parents were set up in one room; the laboring friend and her husband were set up in the other. The layout of the upstairs contained only two bedrooms with a doorway between them, which made it a whole lot easier for the midwife. My mother and her friend labored together and started giving birth at the exact same time. The midwife was running back and forth between the two rooms, while the fathers were delivering us. By the end of the night, two baby girls were born. It was as though we were twins from different parents, and we were forever bonded.

After my birth, my parents decided we would live in a teepee. Of course, I don't remember this, but I remember the stories and have seen the photographs. At this point, my parents had my brother who was two, me, and probably a dog. We lived here for the warmer months of 1979.

One of my favorite stories about the teepee was told to me by my grandmother, my mother's mother. She told me that she thought my father was a nice son-in-law because when she and my grandfather came to visit my father dug my grandmother her very own hole. We didn't have a bathroom in the teepee, of course, so my parents would dig holes to use the bathroom in so it could be buried later. My very considerate father was being hospitable.

While sharing this story with my grandfather, my father's stepfather, he told me a comical story about our teepee that I had never heard. My parents were completely content living in a teepee in the middle of the woods, with two small children, except for one small detail. My parents couldn't keep me from crawling underneath the cloth flooring of the teepee. He also added that we were the happiest and dirtiest little kids he knew. When living in a teepee bathing is not a priority, and when all you know is living in the forest and crawling in the dirt, all the while being loved and cared for, I can understand why we were happy kids.

2 ~ Log Cabin # 1 Tal, Ohio

At some point, I'm not sure when, why, or how, we moved to the same log cabin where I was born. The other family moved somewhere else, but they were still close by. This is where my memories began, but only in bits and pieces. If I were to guess, I would say I was probably two, or rather had my second birthday there. I don't remember my birthday, just the night before. You see, those old log cabins were built very simply, with minimal materials. The bedroom floors were made up of bare wooden planks, missing knotholes, and all. I remember lying on the floor and looking through one of those knotholes watching my mother putting the icing on my birthday cake in the kitchen below. We had a wood-burning stove for cooking and baking, which she must have used to bake the cake earlier that evening. The kitchen was

brightly lit by kerosene lamps
and she was watching something
on the small black and white
television set that was powered
a car battery. As I was
watching my mother through the
knothole, I remember feeling
loved, I remember the warmth,
and I remember feeling slightly
guilty because I was ruining my
surprise birthday cake for the
next day.

My memories are mostly
small and unimportant. For
instance, I remember having a
big wooden barrel to collect
rainwater in. We also had a
grey, long-haired cat named
Libby who had kittens, I
remember an orange one
specifically. In my two-year-
old mind, it seemed like a good
idea to pick up that little
orange kitten and put it in the
barrel. I couldn't see inside
the barrel because I was too
small, so I'm not sure if I knew
it was full of water, but
whether I knew or not the result
was the same. I put a helpless

kitten in a barrel full of rainwater. I wasn't trying to hurt the kitten, but it would have drowned had my four-year-old, and much taller, brother not been there to save the day.

I remember Gerald and I "digging a hole to China" in the dirt next to the cabin, but we never reached our destination. We were also looking for dinosaur bones on our way to China, but never found any. I remember him taking me to the outhouse in the dark, which was out a short path through the woods away from the cabin. We would take turns putting on "light shows" with a flashlight in the woods while the other was using the outhouse. We used a five-gallon bucket for a toilet during the winter so we wouldn't have to hike to the outhouse in the cold. I remember once putting one of my brother's small toy astronauts in this bucket, which was full. I remember doing it on purpose, although not out of malice. I just wanted to see what would happen, cause and effect. The effect was my brother was upset and I got in trouble. I remember sitting on my mother's lap at the kitchen table with the sunshine coming in the windows. She was wearing a peasant top with fuchsia, teal, and purple stripes. I was sitting on her lap backward, my back to her stomach, with my arms above my head and around her neck. I remember sitting on the couch and the kittens jumping up and getting my little feet that were barely hanging over the edge. I remember playing on the back deck with a hammock, trying to wrap myself up with the hammock like I was in a spider web.

We bathed in a tin washtub sometimes, but I also remember bathing in the freezing cold creek at the bottom of our hill. I remember it being a miserable and memorable experience, with so much of an impact that whenever I smell cheap orange shampoo, probably VO5, or something comparable, it instantly takes me back to crying and shivering in the creek while my father was washing my hair. I remember going out in the woods and finding my favorite flower, Princess Lady Slippers, which are very odd-looking flowers with sort of a bubble underneath the petals. The bubbles actually look very similar to testicles. For some reason, I loved to pop those flower bubbles. I knew I wasn't allowed to because "we don't hurt flowers," and they were quite rare, but I just couldn't help it. I remember popping the flowers knowing that I would get in trouble, but I did it anyway, that whole cause and effect thing.

I started having a reoccurring dream in the log cabin, which continued for years. In this dream, my mother, father, brother, and I were in the living room of the log cabin. My parents asked my brother and me if we wanted popcorn. We both said no, so as a consequence my parents used a stapler to staple the skin on the top of our hands. They would put in a staple, twist the skin, put in another staple, and continue until all the skin was twisted and distorted on both of our hands. My brother and I would go upstairs and take each other's staples out while crying. The next day, same situation, we would be in the living room and my parents asked if we wanted popcorn. In this dream, I seemed to have learned my lesson. When offered the popcorn I knew better than to say no. I didn't want my hands stapled again. Gerald did not learn his lesson. He did not want popcorn, so his hands were stapled again. Dream psychology is very fascinating, and this reoccurring dream is very odd. My parents never stapled our hands if we didn't want popcorn, or for any other reason, but I had this exact same dream for years. The details never changed, even down to the dark green flower vase that I was eating popcorn out of while my parents were stapling my brother's hands that second night.

By far, the absolute very best memory I have while living in the log cabin is when my younger sister, Scarlett was born. I turned two in November, and she was born on March 23rd, 1981. It was late, my brother and I were sleeping. My God Mother woke us up to watch. He didn't want to get up, but I sure did. I was excited! I was fascinated by babies and we were getting ready to have one.

As far as the actual birth goes, I don't remember anything. What I do remember, or at least what I think I remember, is a green, slimy bubble coming out of my mother and popping. To this day, I have no idea what that green bubble was, or even if my green bubble memory is accurate, but that's what I remember. My God Mother took me downstairs and read a book to me after my sister was born. I don't remember the story inside, but the cover was black and white zebra stripes. I wish I could remember more details, but then again, I was only two. I was so in love with my baby sister. I called her "our baby." I have always been protective of her ever since she was born. Even though we fought like crazy when we were young, our sisterly love and bond could never be broken.

*** On a side note, after my sister's birth, I started "breastfeeding" my dolls. I would pull up my shirt and hold my "baby" up to my chest so it could eat, which was the only way I knew to feed a baby.

3 ~ The Monster is Born

It amazes me that I have
these vivid memories, I was only
two years old. I'm not sure how
long we lived in this log cabin,
but it couldn't have been too
long, a year or two at the most.
These memories are so vivid, and
so deeply embedded in my brain.
My memories are a blessing, but
they are also a curse. I wish
all my memories were pleasant,
but they're not. This is the
same time the Invisible Monster
first made its ugly appearance.
This memory is quite painful and
terrible. This memory has
caused me a childhood of pain,
and definitely is a contributing
factor to my adult "crazy
brain." This horrible,
terrible, disgusting,
mortifying, and any other bad
words I can throw in, memory is
one that I wish I could
permanently erase. Sadly, it
doesn't work that way.

My brother and I were in the woods, along with another little girl, who was the same age as me. She was a child from one of the log cabin families. While out in the woods Gerald said, "You go first because it's easier." I needed no other explanation. He pulled down his pants and laid on the ground, and I proceeded to suck on his penis. I did this in a completely knowing manner, which means it wasn't the first time it happened, just the first and only time I remember it happening. After we both took turns on him, we switched places and he took his turn on us.

In my memory, Gerald was the initiator. He was older than me, maybe four at the time, but at this point, in my mind, he was still innocent. I don't believe that children are born with this knowledge. I don't begrudge him for that specific experience. It was just a horrible experience that we both shared together. I know I was only two and I had no idea what was happening, but the guilt I feel from this is unimaginable. I don't know why we did it or where we learned it.

These questions have always haunted me. Someone is responsible for this, but who? Someone is to blame for this childhood-trauma. Who is this Invisible Monster? Did my father do something to him, or us both? Did my mother do something to him, or us both? Did they teach us to do this to each other? Or did my brother just see my parents having sex since we did live in such close quarters early on, being the teepee? Did they think we were sleeping and think they were being discrete?

Did this knowledge come from the other little girl who was involved, or her family? Did her father do something to her? This is a possibility. A few years ago, I started doing some research and found a man who I believed to be her father. He was in prison in Ohio for some type of sexual charge with a family member. I even located his photograph. I have no memory whatsoever of what he looked like, only his name, so I couldn't be certain this was her father. I was so relieved. Maybe I found the root cause. Maybe I found the answers I so desperately needed. Maybe with this new information, I could finally move on.

I wanted to be sure this was the same man from our past, so I brought the subject up to my father. I told him what I had discovered through my research. I even had the picture pulled up online to show him. I needed to know if this was the same man, that little girl's father. My father was surprisingly quick to say this was not him. He was so quick to dismiss my inquiry, almost cutting me off in mid-sentence, that I found his reaction alarmingly odd. This alarmingly odd reaction, once again, raised the question, was my father the one who caused this? Is he the Invisible Monster?

These questions, I know, will never be answered. These questions are one of the many reasons I can never trust my parents. The only thing I know for certain is that something did happen, somehow, somewhere, which effectively ruined my brother. Someone took away his chance for a healthy childhood. I hate whoever did this to him! I hate whoever did this to us! Not only did it ruin my brother, but it also caused severe, lifelong damage to me, as well as many other future victims. Someone took away our chance for a healthy childhood. I will always have this Invisible Monster haunting me. What an incredible burden to bear.

4 ~ Log Cabin # 2 Tal, Ohio

The time after that is foggy. Although I don't remember it happening, I know that my mother left. My father, my brother, my sister, and I moved to another log cabin. I think the cabin belonged to a friend who was no longer using it. I don't remember the cabin at all, just the outside area. I remember a fire pit where we would cook, but the only reason I remember the fire pit area is that I remember getting ready to eat macaroni and cheese, which was cooked over the fire. It was my job to stir the powdered cheese and butter into the fire-cooked pasta. My brother's job was to pour cups of milk, Styrofoam cups, to go along with dinner. He thought it would be funny to poke a hole in the bottom of my cup. After pouring my milk he handed it to me. Holding my cup in my hand, I cried as I watched the milk slowly leak through the small hole.

This log cabin didn't have an outhouse, per se. It was more of a platform on stilts, with a hole in the middle for a seat. There were no walls, and it was in an open, flat area. Other than the few steps leading up to the platform, underneath was fully exposed. My brother and I would take turns watching each other poop from behind the platform. I guess we were playing "midwife" because we would act like our poop was a baby coming out. Gerald would say, "I can see it, the baby's coming." Isolated forest kids and their imagination!

One morning, outside the log cabin, I heard someone crying down by the creek at the bottom of the hill. I walked down and saw my father sitting on a rock crying so hard he was shaking. When he realized I was there he stopped crying. He scooped me up off the ground and cradled me like a baby. He looked at me with a smile on his face and said, "Your eyes are as blue as the sky." Those words have always stuck in my mind. I'm not even sure why. Maybe the tender, loving way he spoke to me, to love me when he was in such pain. In my adult mind I can only assume my father was crying over my mother leaving, and the fact that his marriage was ending. He lost the love of his life. He once told me that he will never find someone he's more compatible with than he was with my mother. I think he will always be in love with the person she was, but I will strongly stress the WAS.

5 ~ One Room Schoolhouse
Southern Ohio (somewhere)

Our next house was a renovated one-room schoolhouse right next to a small, very old cemetery. I use the word "renovated" loosely. It was in very rough shape, but it did have two bedrooms petitioned off. I'm pretty sure my mother lived there, too, at first. There was a trail into the woods, behind the house which my father placed our handmade clubhouse. My father was a skilled carpenter and had previously built an amazing tall wooden platform that felt as high as the trees when I was small. The platform had railings all the way around, minus the opening for the ladder, and underneath had railings with window openings. It was the perfect area for little girls to play "house." Thankfully we were able to move it from the log cabin to our new house. I have a vague memory of my mother lying on that platform, drinking coffee and reading a book in the sunshine, which is the only memory I have of her there. I turned four when we lived in this house. I celebrated my birthday with that same little girl I was born with, and we both got red t-shirts with our name on the front and the number four on the back.

I have quite a few memories there, and most were good, although I did receive my first set of stitches while living there, courtesy of my brother. It was purely a wrong place at the wrong time kind of thing, and I also should add, they were just butterfly stitches. Gerald had drawn an airplane on his Etch A Sketch, and he was obviously proud of his drawing. He showed me and asked me if I liked it. I have no idea why I said it, but I answered, "No." I'm sure it was a very nice airplane, but I said no anyways.

I don't know if I wanted to look again and change my answer, because saying no wasn't very nice, but I leaned over to get a second look. This second look just happened to be when he started to shake the Etch A Sketch to erase the perfectly fine airplane. He was just trying to erase it, but I hurt his feelings, so he was shaking a little more aggressively than necessary; the inside of my left eyebrow caught the edge of the Etch A Sketch. As I said, wrong place at the wrong time.

We lived in this house around Halloween. I was scared to death of the cemetery because Gerald told me that after it got dark on Halloween witches would come out of the cemetery. I remember lying awake and not taking my eyes off the window. I know that's just one of those things brothers do, but that cemetery was creepy enough to live next door to without an older brother to torment you on top of it. The cemetery was one of those really old ones that you could barely make out the words on the headstones. There was an old wrought iron, very rough-looking fence surrounding the cemetery, and the grounds were long overgrown. So yeah, the story about the witches didn't help.

This house was situated on a fairly busy road, and there weren't too many houses around. When we went trick-or-treating that year, we just did it at home. It's possible we didn't have a car to drive somewhere else, I'm not really sure, but for whatever reason, my father decided we would do it at home. My siblings and I all got dressed up in our costumes. My father stayed in the house to pass out candy. We would go to the front door, knock, say, "Trick-or-treat," and my father would give us each candy. Then we would go to the back door, knock, say, "Trick-or-treat," and my father would give us more candy. We did this all evening,

front door, back door, front
door, back door. My father
always had clever ideas like
this to make sure we had fun.

My father started jogging
and we were too small to stay
home alone, so my father would
tie a rope around his waist. He
would then tie the rope to my
brother's Big Wheel bike, then
tie it to my Big Wheel bike, and
last but not least, tie the end
of the rope to my sister's
miniature Big Wheel bike. I'm
sure it was a comical sight
watching my father run down the
road pulling us behind him like
a train. I remember finding a
little chipmunk with a broken
leg on one of these trips. It
was still alive, and we wanted
to try to save it. My Big Wheel
bike was a Smurf bike with a
Smurf head on the front. This
Smurf head was the perfect place
to lay the injured chipmunk so
we could take it home. My
father ran home, pulling us all
behind him, chipmunk included.

We couldn't save the chipmunk,
but we tried.

I know my father did the
best he could for us at the
time. What choice did he have?
My mother left him alone with
three small children. I don't
remember being sad about my
mother leaving, but I know I
was. I once remember throwing a
fit so bad I actually injured my
father. I remember the fit, but
I didn't remember why I was
upset. I later asked my father
about it and he said I was
crying because I wanted my
"mommy." We were sitting in our
car outside of my preschool. I
think we were going to an open
house, or something because it
was dark outside. We had an old
station wagon with the kind of
seatbelts that hung from the
ceiling between the front seats.
When these seatbelts weren't
buckled, they were just hanging
there, loose, with a big metal
buckle at the end. I was in the
back seat and my father was in
the driver's seat, turned around

facing me. In my fit of rage, I grabbed the seatbelt and flung it forward, smacking him in the forehead with the buckle. It was dark so I couldn't see what I had done. My father turned the car light on to show me the blood running down his face. I felt so horrible. I wasn't trying to hurt him; I was just upset. My father didn't yell at me. He didn't punish me. He only comforted me. His physical injury was nothing compared to the pain he felt from his little girl wanting her mommy. Then we went inside and ate chocolate-covered bananas. It's funny the details that stick in your mind, chocolate-covered bananas.

It would be safe to say I was not dealing well with my mother's departure. I remember throwing the biggest fit another time because my father had given me a dollar. I'm not sure why he was giving it to me, but I remember he told me it was mine. I told him it wasn't mine. I didn't want the dollar, but I'm not sure why. My father kept telling me it was mine and I would argue to say that it wasn't mine. This went back and forth for a few rounds so I decided to finalize it. After stating once more the dollar wasn't mine, I tore that one-dollar bill into tiny little pieces. I have no idea why I was so dead set on not accepting the dollar, or why my father was intent on giving me the dollar. What I do know is that we were so poor that my father patiently taped the tiny little pieces of that one-dollar bill back together, and then kept the dollar for himself.

At this time my mother was living back in Kettering near her parents and siblings. Her goal was to go back home and get settled so we would be able to live with her. She did get settled, but it was into another relationship. My mother and her new boyfriend, my future stepfather, moved in together almost instantly. The first

time I met him my mother brought
him with her to pick us up for a
visit. I'm sure that wasn't
very pleasant for my father.

6 ~ Kettering, Ohio (somewhere)

I don't remember the transition, but at some point, my siblings and I moved in with my mother and her boyfriend, Stuart. They had a very small one-bedroom apartment. We slept on a pull-out couch in the living room, which was fine. We were still pretty small, Gerald was six, I was four, and Scarlett was two. Stuart had a daughter, Ashley, from a previous marriage. She was a year younger than me and a year older than Scarlett. She lived with her mother, so we only saw her on weekends.

Ashley fit right in with us, and we were extremely happy to have another kid to play with. I even remember her favorite game. She always wanted to play princesses, which was fine with my sister and me, but Ashley was always quick to say, "I get to be the oldest and

the prettiest."   We had
extremely different
personalities than she did so it
would never even have crossed
our minds to call being the
"oldest" and the "prettiest."
But we were still slightly
disappointed. I remember
saying, "That's not fair,
Ashley. You always get to be the
oldest and the prettiest."
Kids…

My mother worked as a
bartender at a local bar, White
Sail. It was a small bar, and
my mother knew the owner outside
of work. The owner would
eventually become my cousin's
father, but the only thing I
remember about him is that he
had a van with a Star Wars scene
painted on the side that we
played in. Usually, Stuart
watched us while she was
working. I use the words,
"watched us," very loosely
though. It was more like he
sent us outside and we weren't
allowed to come in until my
mother was there. I think he

usually was sleeping, but I'm not positive.

With that lack of supervision, my two-year-old sister once found mushrooms under a tree and decided to eat them. That's what you do with mushrooms, right? You eat them? Four-year-old me recognized the danger of the situation and woke up Stuart. He didn't take her to the hospital. He instead, called my mother at work. My mother was able to get a prescription for Scarlett that would make her throw up the mushrooms. My sister was fine, but she learned a valuable lesson. Do not eat wild mushrooms.

Quite often we would go to work with my mother, I think. Or maybe she just took us there when she was off so she could drink and hang out. Either way, we spent a lot of time at the White Sail. The parking lot of White Sail is actually where we would play in the Star Wars van.

The van was so cool! Besides
the Star Wars scene painted on
the outside, the inside was
pretty cool, too. It was one of
those old camper/vans that had a
little kitchenette, table, bed,
and even a toilet inside if I
remember correctly.

We were usually only there
during the day, but there were
always at least a couple people
sitting at the bar. Every once
in a while, my mother would be a
little more drunk than usual so
we would be there in the early
evening. The rule was if the
bar gets crowded go sit at the
end of the bar and be quiet. We
loved going there though.
Sometimes people would give us
quarters to play the arcade
games. I'm sure it was somebody
who felt sorry for us since we
were little kids hanging out in
a bar, or some guy trying to get
in my mother's pants. We didn't
care though. We got quarters,
and we liked playing the games.
There was a bowling game I
particularly liked. If the bar

was empty, we were allowed to use the pool table. Sometimes we would get a pack of Wrigley's Spearmint Gum. If we were really lucky, we might get a bag of chips. We did, however, have an unlimited supply of "bar pop." I say, "bar pop," because all "bar pop" tastes the same, or at least I thought so when I was smaller. I'm not even sure what that particular taste is, maybe it was just the combination of cigarette smoke, the smell of alcohol, and the taste of the actual pop. It's not just a fountain drink thing, because I've had plenty of fountain drinks in my day and they have never tasted like "bar pop" unless I'm at a bar. White Sail was the first bar I ever frequented.

My father was still living in the one-room schoolhouse in southern Ohio. Once while visiting, I'm not exactly sure why, he felt he had to put a disposable diaper on me to sleep. I had not worn a diaper in a long time, and I had never worn a disposable diaper, only a cloth diaper. But for whatever reason, he felt I needed it. He laid me down on the diaper, so I peed. He hadn't even closed it up yet, I just peed. It was a conscious decision; I knew exactly what I was doing. That's what you do in diapers, right? My father got mad and asked me why I did that, and my answer was exactly that. "You are supposed to pee in diapers." He never put a diaper on me again. Profound reverse psychology from the mind of a four-year-old?

7 ~ Culver Avenue # 1
Kettering, Ohio

It's funny that I can always remember my age because of where I lived. By the time I was 14 I had already lived in 15 different places, so it only makes sense I can figure out my age by where I lived. When I was five, turning six we lived in a small house in Kettering within walking distance to my grandparents, my mother's parents. I don't think we lived there very long. The house was very small but had three bedrooms, my sister and I shared a bedroom, along with our soon-to-be stepsister on the weekends. The house had a dishwasher and I remember being fascinated by it. I was still adjusting to electricity, running water, and indoor plumbing.

I have one very strange memory here. It must have been

a weekend because Ashley was there. Scarlett was still in a crib, and Ashley and I shared a mattress on the floor. I woke up in the middle of the night to find her placing stuffed animals all around me, making a circle. She was whispering, or chanting rather, while she was encircling me with these stuffed animals. She didn't know I woke up. I just peaked at her when she wasn't looking to see what she was doing, and it was very strange. It almost felt like she was worshiping me, or something equally disturbing. As far as I know, Ashley didn't know that I woke up that evening, nor have I ever asked her about it. It was just one of those things that happened.

I have a less significant, but equally amusing, memory of playing with Barbies in my bedroom with Scarlett and Ashely. I have no idea how my sister came up with the idea, but she said, "Look, if I rub my finger on Barbie's butt it really smells like butt," then proceeded to rub Barbie's butt. She then held her finger up for Ashley and me to smell. We both had the same reaction, "Ooh, gross. It really does smell like butt." Why did Barbie's butt really smell like butt? It shouldn't, she's just a doll. It didn't make any sense. Later that day my sister told me a little secret. She said, "I rubbed my butt before I rubbed Barbie's butt. I was just tricking you." The things kids do......

I don't believe we saw my father very often during this time, but he did come to pick us up on occasion. On one of those occasions, my father took us to his sister's house for a visit. My aunt had small children, so we loved going there to play with our cousins. After a lovely visit, we piled into the front cab of my father's truck to leave. My brother was sitting next to my father, then me, then my sister closest to

the door. Back then booster
seats and seatbelts weren't the
norm, but what happened next is
a very good example of why they
are now. As we turned the first
corner the truck door flew open.
Scarlett fell out, landing on
the road, and rolling like a log
right alongside the truck. My
sister was next to me, and then
she was gone. Luckily, she
escaped with only bumps and
bruises, and from that point
forward my brother sat by the
door.

8 ~ Culver Avenue # 2
Kettering, Ohio

After a brief time in the small house on Culver we moved to a house directly across the street, but still on Culver. The house was bigger, the yard was nicer, and we had the most beautiful, covered porch. Actually, I'm sure it was quite junky, but I loved it. I'm sure my mother tried to make it nice with her house plants. My favorite thing in the world was to sit out on that porch during thunderstorms. I loved it! I loved the sound. I loved the way the air felt. I loved the energy of the lightning. I loved the rumble of the thunder which I felt all the way through to the pit of my stomach. These extreme feelings I felt at that young age have never gone away. I love thunderstorms with a passion, and I long for a beautiful, covered porch so I can be out in the storms once again.

This house was slightly larger, but not large enough. My siblings and I all shared a room.   After my sister fell asleep one night my brother decided it would be a good idea if we played a game, but he got to make up the rules. Reluctantly I agreed, and then he told me the rules. The rules were, he would pull his first layer of clothing off, and then I had to go. I didn't want to play this game, but he told me I had to. He took off his pants but left his underwear on. Then it was my turn. I remember saying, "That's not fair. You have on pants and underwear. I'm just wearing a nightgown and underwear." But he got to make up the rules, so he made me take my underwear off. He then made me bend over on all fours, into a crawling position. I didn't want to do it, but I did it anyway. I'm not sure why I didn't fight harder. Luckily,

right at that moment, my mother
came into our room. I'm afraid
to think of what would have
happened if she hadn't. She
told us to stop and go to bed,
so we did. It was never
mentioned again. It was as if
it never happened, like it
wasn't a big deal. This was a
big deal! It should have been
addressed, but it wasn't. Why?
Could my mother be the Invisible
Monster?

On many different
occasions, a little memory will
pop into my head. I'll have a
flashback of something that
seemed insignificant at the
time, or normal, or whatever you
want to call it. But in my
adult mind, it becomes one of
those "what the fuck" moments.
When I was in Kindergarten my
mother decided it a good idea to
try on her new sexy, black, very
sheer, lingerie she was planning
on wearing for Stuart later that
evening, which is fine, of
course. What is not fine is
modeling the sexy, black, very

sheer lingerie for my brother and me, then asking what we think. And I would like to stress the very sheer, as in very, very, very sheer. There wasn't a thing we couldn't see. I would probably understand more if she had just shown me, being a girl and all, but that was extremely inappropriate for her to model that lingerie for her son. Don't get me wrong, a mother shouldn't try on her lingerie for her six-year daughter either, but her eight-year-old son? Is this the Invisible Monster rearing its ugly head? Is my mother the Invisible Monster?

My mother and Stuart decided to get a puppy, and we were so happy. We hadn't had a pet in a little while, and we were used to having at least one dog, and maybe a cat. He was a beautiful dog, blonde, short hair, but built like a German Shepard. We named him Loki, pronounced with a long I. I don't remember much about him, other than that he was a puppy and did puppy things. My brother had the responsibility of being the pooper scooper. I remember being thankful it wasn't my responsibility. Loki was a puppy, you know, doing puppy things. I can't say what Loki specifically did, but he did something that sent Stuart into a blind rage. He picked that poor puppy up and slammed him into the front door. Loki's head hit the door hard and he was obviously injured. He could barely get up, and his eyes were crossed. That poor puppy was ruined that day. He survived the head injury, but he wasn't quite right. Later my mother took him to be put to sleep after biting a little girl. It wasn't a bad bite, but bad enough to know it wasn't a safe dog to have around her children.

I really don't want to give the impression that my entire life was terrible and horrible. I was actually a fairly happy child, at least as far as I remember. We were always going camping or going on fishing trips with groups of friends. I know alcohol and drugs were definitely part of the fun for the adults, but we had a lot of fun too. There was always a large group of kids that came along with those adults. We would stay up late, roast marshmallows, tell ghost stories, and whatever other fun things you do on camping and fishing trips. My mother was always a ton of fun on these trips and had the best ghost stories. She seemed to know everything about plant life, what was edible, what was definitely not edible, and she always felt it was important to pass on this information to us. I loved the knowledge she gave me during these trips, and a lot of that knowledge is still there, deep down in memories.

Around this same time, my mother and Stuart decided to get married. I have grown up watching a video of these

newlyweds at my grandparents'
house. In this video, the
camera zooms in on my mother and
him, each with a beer in their
hand, and my grandfather
introduces them as newlyweds.
My grandfather asks the
newlyweds if they are going to
have any more children. They
both say no with such conviction
that it is painfully obvious
they did not want any additions
to their new family. My mother
was already pregnant with Dani,
but she didn't know.

9 ~ Baby Girl

Dani was born on October 18th, 1985, and I fell in love. I loved that baby girl deeper than I knew I could love. I turned eight the November after Dani was born, but even at that young age, I had discovered my purpose in life. I was to love and protect Dani like she was my own, somebody had to. I truly felt as though Dani was my baby and I never wanted to leave her side.

Shortly after Dani was born her father went to prison in Terre Haute, Indiana. I think it was something to do with cocaine, and I am pretty sure it was a charge from before he met my mother. At least that's what my eight-year-old mind remembers. Regardless of how, when, or why, he did go to prison for a while, and my mother was left to raise four and a half kids on her own.

Ashley would still come on weekends even though her father was in prison. I remember visiting him there a few times, and to this day that prison in Terre Haute is the only prison I have ever set foot in. I pray that it will also be my last.

I didn't really mind that my stepfather was in prison. I actually rather liked it. He was a scary man. I do remember him being nice sometimes, but overall, I was scared of him. He had the evilest eyes I'd ever seen on a person. Once, before he went to prison, I think while my mother was pregnant with Dani, he came in one evening. I think he had been at a bar or something. I don't remember him saying anything, but he was definitely angry. He went straight to the kitchen and grabbed a butcher knife, then started to leave. My mother tried to stop him, but he just pushed past her and left anyway. I thought he killed someone with that knife that evening when I

was little, but who knows what
really happened after he left.

10 ~ Hank's Pub

During Stuart's prison sentence my mother started her downward spiral, or maybe she was already there, and I was just too young to realize it. My mother spent all her time at another local bar called Hank's Pub, with her newborn infant in tow. This was the second bar I frequented. I liked going to Hank's Pub better than White Sail. The layout of the bar was better for kids. At Hank's Pub, there was a backroom away from the bar area, and we were to stay back there. Unless, of course, my mother got extra drunk and we stayed at the bar up into the evening, then we had to sit at the bar quietly until she was ready to leave. We loved going there though. Once again, we were given quarters for the arcade games by the "drunks" that felt sorry for us. The same scenario as before, just a different bar, we had an

unlimited supply of "bar pop,"
and if we were lucky someone
would buy us chips. Hank's Pub
was a dart bar, so we were able
to play darts if we were the
only ones there. There was a
soft pretzel bakery across the
street we were allowed to go to
if it was early enough, and if
we had money. You could
actually watch the pretzels
being made there, start to
finish, and you could buy them
fresh out of the oven, soft and
warm. They were delicious!

Hank's Pub had a jukebox
that we loved playing music on.
Some of my favorite childhood
songs were songs I heard at the
bar, songs like "Patience" by
Guns N' Roses, "Nothing Compares
2U" by Sinead O'Connor, and
"What I Am (Shove me in the
shallow water, before I get too
deep)" by Edie Brickell & New
Bohemians. And don't forget
"Open Arms" by Journey, that was
one that caused a hush over the
bar as it seemed to invoke
something deeply within the

drunken bargoers. I remember
dancing to Paula Abdul's
"Straight Up" and Bobby Brown's
"Every Little Step I Take" in
the front of the bar with my
sister, Scarlett. We felt like
we were on stage with the
spotlight shining on us, and
everyone was watching. The
lights were actually shining on
the dartboards behind us. But
we had fun dancing, and the
bargoers seemed to enjoy it,
applauding when we were done.

If it was nice out, we were
allowed to go outside and play
in the small grass area behind
Hank's Pub. There was also a
little creek to play in. This
was all normal to us. Don't all
kids spend time their playing in
creeks behind bars? A bargoer
once noticed us playing and was
absolutely horrified by what we
were doing. You see, I found an
old syringe near the creek and I
picked it up. I'm sure someone
had shot up heroin, or
something, with that syringe and
threw it in the creek before

they went into the bar. And I
was playing with it! A stray
dog had come from somewhere and
I was pretending to give the dog
shots. The actual needle wasn't
in the syringe, so I wasn't
really sticking the dog. I
didn't realize how messed up
that was at the time, but
looking back now, "Oh my
freakin' goodness."

Dani spent the most time
with my mother at Hank's Pub by
far. My siblings and I were in
school during the day, but Dani
was just a baby. My mother
carried her on her back in one
of those backpack baby carriers.
She was still pretty young so
she would mostly sleep, and my
mother would sit at the bar and
drink. With only a small baby
strapped to her back, and her
other kids in school, my mother
could sit at the bar as long as
she wanted to, at least until
school got out. Looking back,
it's crazy how any bar anywhere
would allow something like that.

Late one evening, my mother was at Hank's Pub with Dani on her back. My siblings and I were with our aunt and uncle, my father's sister, so Dani wasn't with us. I guess we had stayed the night with them, or something. They tried to take us home, but my mother wasn't there. I don't remember that part, but I do remember being in the parking lot at Hank's Pub. My mother had Dani strapped to her back like usual. She was so drunk. She wanted my aunt and uncle to leave us with her at the bar. I remember a bunch of yelling. I remember my aunt not letting us get out of the car. We drove off with my mother standing there, with Dani on her back. I was so upset. I couldn't understand why we didn't take Dani, too.

11 ~ Covington, Ohio (somewhere)

My mother moved towards her family when my parents split up. My father did the opposite and moved farther away from his family. I'm not sure how my father decided on Covington, Ohio, but that's where he ended up. My father was living with a girlfriend and they were regularly attending NA meetings together. She was nice, she wore a lot of jewelry, and she had a son who had curly red hair. Other than that, I really don't remember her much, but I know I liked her, or maybe I just liked the fact that she paid attention to me.

My father picked us up for a visit once and we stopped at a gas station on the way to his girlfriend's house. He thought it would be fun to buy each of us a scratch-off lottery ticket. We'd never had a lottery ticket before, so it was rather

exciting. It was especially
exciting when I won a dollar
with my lottery ticket. I was
so happy. I won! With my
winnings, I asked my father to
buy me another scratch-off
lottery ticket. He bought me
the ticket. I scratched it off,
and nothing. This ticket was
not a winning lottery ticket,
and I lost my dollar. This was
a deeply ingrained life lesson
for me. I have never been one
to gamble and I'm pretty sure
this experience is why. I won a
dollar, I gambled with it, I
lost it.

12 ~ It Gives Me Character

When I was seven my sister
and I were visiting our father
over Easter break. My brother
wasn't with us, but I'm not sure
why. My father and his
girlfriend had taken us to an NA
meeting which was being held in
a church. My sister and I were
supposed to stay downstairs and
play in the nursery. We were
used to playing alone so we
really didn't mind, but we kept
going upstairs to peek at the NA
meeting that was taking place.
My father noticed us and got up
to tell us to stay downstairs.
We ran downstairs and hid from
my father, in a playful way. I
decided to hide under the crib
that was in the nursery. When I
was younger I had really long,
blonde hair, and it kept getting
tangled in the springs on the
bottom of the crib, so I looked
for another place to hide. I
found the perfect hiding place
behind the nursery door. The

nursery was the only room
located at the bottom of a
stairwell, immediately to the
left with a door that opened
outwards. When the door was
open it was against the wall at
the bottom of the stairs. It
was the perfect hiding spot, or
so I thought.

As I was ducking behind the
door, in my perfect hiding spot,
I was able to see up the stairs.
From my perfect hiding spot, I
was able to see the glass doors
that were the main entrance of
the church, and the landing at
the top of the stairs. I saw my
father on the landing, so I
crouched down even tighter
behind the door in anticipation.
He never made his way down to
tell us to behave because a
large man came through the main
entrance doors and stopped him.
I didn't recognize this man, but
he went straight up to my
father. As I watched from my
perfect hiding spot, I saw this
large man and my father hugging.
Everyone hugs at NA meetings, so

I didn't think it was strange. My father was then shoved down the stairs and crashed into the door at the bottom, my perfect hiding spot. Since I was behind the door, crouching down, my face was exactly the same level as the doorknob, my right eye to be exact, and the back of my head was up against the wall. My right eyebrow was instantly split open from the force of the doorknob, causing a large skin flap to hang loosely above my eye. My face was smashed between the doorknob and a wall. I screamed "MOMMY!" at the top of my lungs and then peed my pants. My father scooped me up and ran to the bathroom to get paper towels to try to stop the bleeding. As he was holding me in his arms, frantically grabbing paper towels I saw myself in the mirror. I was covered in blood from head to toe, my entire face, my clothes, my hair, everything. When you're seven years old and you see yourself completely covered in blood that image tends to stick with you for life.

My father and his girlfriend rushed me to the car to take me to the hospital. My father was driving, and I was sitting on his girlfriend's lap. I remember her whispering a question in my ear, "Did you pee your pants?" I did and I'm sure I was getting pee on her lap, but she didn't care. She just hugged me tighter. My father was driving frantically, running red lights, and putting us at risk, so she convinced him to pull over and let her drive. I rode the rest of the way in my father's lap, with my wet pants.

When we got to the hospital, I was taken back to a room immediately. I don't remember crying. I don't remember pain. I just remember sitting there with my father keeping pressure on the wound. It seemed like we had to wait forever to see a doctor. I think the doctor was out for a jog and we had to wait for him to get back, but I have no idea why I think that. It's just what I've always thought. When I was finally examined by a doctor it was obvious that I would need stitches. I was taken into another room where I was strapped down on a board. The straps covered my whole body from my neck down, and it was so tight. I wasn't able to fully expand my lungs. I told them I couldn't breathe, but they said I had to stay strapped in so I wouldn't move. I knew I wouldn't move if they let me out. I just wanted to breathe. I guess in their experience most kids aren't as brave as I was. They should have known that I was brave by the fact that they never even saw me cry. I was completely calm the entire time, but they thought they knew best.

Once I was trapped, I mean strapped to board I was told I was going to be given a shot. I was told it would feel like a bee sting. I felt the slight

pinch of the shot that they
compared to a bee sting, and I
remember thinking, "Well, that
didn't feel like a bee sting at
all." The location of the wound
was in the middle of my right
eyebrow and was shaped like a
semi-circle, or half of a
doorknob, that started on my
forehead about half an inch
above my eyebrow, down through
my eyebrow, to half an inch
below my eyebrow. My cheekbone
was also chipped, but we didn't
find out about that until later.
They only addressed the obvious
wound. I don't remember them
cleaning the wound, but I'm sure
they did. They placed some type
of drape over my face, only
leaving my right eyebrow
exposed. If I looked up and to
the right, I could still see,
somewhat, and I was able to
watch the doctor stitching me
up, or at least what his hands
were doing. I watched the
entire time he was working, and
I was intrigued. I wasn't
scared at all. I just watched
his hands work, pulling the

stitches through and snipping
them off with small scissors.
After I was stitched up and
bandaged up, I was given a red
popsicle and sent me home.

I still don't remember any
pain with this injury, only the
initial fear at the point of
impact and the fear from seeing
myself covered in blood in the
mirror. I know there had to be
pain. My face was crushed
between a doorknob and a wall.
I was given some type of pill
capsules from the hospital that
my father's girlfriend dissolved
in applesauce. I'm not sure if
I was able to swallow pills at
that point, but she didn't think
I could. And maybe I don't
remember pain because those pill
capsules were pain medication,
but I really don't know. I was
also given some type of ointment
at the hospital. I hated that
ointment. My entire eye had
swollen shut. It was black and
the size of a golf ball. My
father's girlfriend had to pry
my swollen eyelid open and put

that ointment directly on my eyeball. My face had actually swollen all the way down to the middle of my right cheek. We went to church the following Sunday, Easter Sunday, and everyone was staring at me. I guess it's not every day you see a little girl with half her face covered in bandages at church.

When my father brought me back to my mother, after our visit, my mother was outside working in the garden. I talked to her on the telephone after the accident and I remember telling her it wasn't that bad. I wasn't trying to protect her; I really didn't think it was that bad. She saw me from a distance and was horrified. That was the first time she had seen me since my injury, and I guess it must have been quite a sight. She just started crying. I felt at the time she was over-reacting because I didn't think my injury was that bad. It didn't even hurt.

My face looked so horrible, for so long, that my elementary school teacher reported concerns to Child Protective Services. My face was swollen and bruised for months, so there was true concern on my teacher's part. My mother was visited by a social worker, but it was dismissed instantly. I wasn't even with my mother when this injury happened, and it wasn't due to abuse at all. I was just in the wrong place at the wrong time, again. My mother did, however, take me to the doctor to find out why I wasn't healing. My face was x-rayed in the doctor's office and I was given a vision test. My vision was fine, but my x-ray was not. Apparently, I had broken/chipped my cheekbone. I'm not sure why I wasn't x-rayed in the hospital immediately following my injury, but I wasn't. The doctor was focusing on the bleeding wound from the doorknob and nothing else. The force of the doorknob pushed my head back at such an angle that it perfectly exposed

my cheekbone to the edge of the
door, below the doorknob. By
the time my broken/chipped
cheekbone was discovered it was
too late for any treatment, not
that they could have done
anything before it was
discovered, but it would have
been nice to know. I just had a
small piece of bone floating
around in my face until it
eventually absorbed into my
body, I guess. I do however
have a scar for life, but I
don't mind. It gives me
character.

13 ~ Wilmington Pike
Dayton, Ohio

During the time my stepfather was in prison we to move to Dayton, Ohio. Kettering is a nice place with good schools. Dayton is not a nice place and does not have nice schools. This was the first time we lived in Dayton. While living there, my siblings and I were all in elementary school. My brother was in fifth grade, I was in third grade, and my sister was in first grade. We all went to different elementary schools. I never quite understood that. My brother's school had third grade and first grade, so my sister and I could have gone there. My sister's school had third grade and fifth grade, so my brother and I could have gone there. My school was third grade only, which was also strange. I think in the Dayton Public School District all the students' names are placed in a hat and randomly drawn for each school, or something equally ridiculous. There was no consideration when it came to keeping siblings in the same school. However ridiculous it was, my mother couldn't afford to live in Kettering while Stuart was in prison.

Although we lived in Dayton our house was actually really nice. The entire upstairs was converted into a huge bedroom which my sisters and I all shared. My mother and my brother had bedrooms down-stairs. Scarlett and I had bunk beds; Dani was still in a crib. More often than not I would end up in the crib with her though. I couldn't bring her into my bed because I had the top bunk, and it wouldn't have been safe. So, whenever she cried at night I would climb into the crib and wrap my arms around her until she fell back asleep. Dani learned at a very young age that if she needed to be comforted, I would be there for her. As I said earlier, I felt that my sole purpose in life was to love and comfort that little baby girl.

My experience with my other sister was completely different when we lived here. She had a problem with wetting the bed for quite a while. At the time I thought she was just such a heavy sleeper that she didn't wake up when she had to pee. I know now it's a sign of sexual abuse. She had rubber sheets to protect the mattress because she wet the bed almost every night. I don't think I mentioned that there was only one bathroom in this house, and it was on the first floor, we were on the second. I promise I only did it once, or at least only once that I remember. One night I really had to pee, and I was so tired. I didn't want to go all the way downstairs to the bathroom. She peed the bed anyway, right? And she did have rubber sheets, right? It seemed like a good idea at the time, so I climbed down the ladder and got into her bed. I lifted my nightgown, squatted down, and peed on her bed. I didn't do it to be mean. I didn't pee on her, just on her bed, kind of off to the side. I just really didn't want to go downstairs. She peed the bed anyway, right?

I probably should add that we did have a new dog named Sheena. Sheena would stand at the bottom of the stairs that led to our bedroom and bark every time we tried to come down. I don't remember her being a mean dog. Maybe she was just playing with us, but I remember being afraid to come down the stairs if she was down there. So maybe, just maybe, that was one of my rationalizations of why peeing in Scarlett's bed was okay, just maybe.

After the first few years of school being in Kettering, Dayton Public Schools were a whole different world than we were used to. I can't comment too much on my brother's experience. I only know that it was bad. I'm pretty sure he was bullied there. He was an awkward, shy, white boy thrown into Dayton Public Schools. My brother had only gone to a tiny, little country kindergarten when we lived in the one-room schoolhouse, and then Tara Elementary School through fourth grade. I will admit that he was an awkward, shy, white boy at Tara, as well. The only difference was everyone else was white too. Needless to say, he did not do well while living in Dayton.

I can't comment much on my sister's first exposure to Dayton Public Schools either. I know she didn't do well. I do, however, remember her bus stop being a few blocks away from my bus stop. My brother's bus stop was right across the street from mine. But my sister, the little, slightly immature, first-grader had to walk down a

few blocks to a very busy road.
She was okay though, I thought.
She would just sit on the steps
of the bar that was on the same
corner as her bus stop. I
believe the bar was called The
Tank. It never occurred to me
at the time but that was
probably not the very best
location for a bus stop for any
first-grader, let alone my
sister who always seemed to be
off in her own world. At least
The Tank was not open for
business in the morning when the
bus would pick her up, but they
were open in the afternoon when
she was dropped off.

I remember my mother making
comments here and there about
The Tank not being the best
location for her six-year-old
daughter to get on the school
bus, but never to anybody
important, or at least anybody
who could potentially make a
difference. I'm sure it was
just her having a drunken
conversation with one of her
drunk friends, at someone's

house or maybe the bar. She never called anyone significant to express concern for her daughter's safety or well-being. She never made any attempt to have her bus stop moved to a safer, more appropriate location. My mother actually went into The Tank to have a few beers "just to see what it was like," and to see if she it was okay for my sister's bus stop to be there. My mother liked The Tank and decided "they were good people," so it was a perfectly safe place for Scarlett to have her bus stop there while in first grade.

I can, however, make plenty of comments about my first exposure to Dayton Public Schools. In the three Dayton Public Schools that I have gone to white people were always the minority, but I never felt out of place. I was quiet, but friendly. I was a very small girl, and still small to this day, but I was also very, very pretty. I don't want to come across as someone who is full of themselves, I promise, I'm not. I was just a very pretty, petite, little white girl with long, blonde hair down to my waist. I had high cheekbones, and beautifully shaped blueish, greenish, greyish eyes, that would change with what I was wearing on any given day. People used to tell me I looked like a porcelain doll. I had nice, delicate features, a pale complexion, and nicely shaped naturally red lips. Again, my point is not to sound conceited, or snobby, or shallow. My point only is to explain why my transition into Dayton Public School went a little more smoothly than that of my siblings. As it turned out, black people loved me. I was a tiny, little, pretty, white girl with long blonde hair with a pleasant personality. I was easily accepted.

I remember one little black boy who liked me a little more than he should have in third

grade. I don't remember his
name or very many details about
him. I know he was a small,
scraggly, black boy that was
wearing an all-blue sweatsuit.
It wasn't navy blue, more of a
royal blue, but the blue
sweatsuit stands out in my mind,
nonetheless. We were having a
Valentine's Day party at school
so I believe I would have been
around ten by then. I assume we
were all told to bring some type
of snack or treat for the party.
I say we were told to bring
something because my mother was
never the type of mother that
volunteered to do anything nice,
or considerate, or be involved
period with anything to do with
our school unless it was
mandatory, and sometimes not
even then. I brought Twizzlers.
I've always loved Twizzlers. As
I'm passing out my Twizzlers to
all the students in my class,
placing them on the plates that
have been provided, this small,
scraggly, black boy wearing the
blue sweatsuit came up behind
me. He patted my butt, and gave

a little squeeze, and whispered
in my ear from behind, in
probably the best romantic voice
he could muster, you know, being
in third grade and all, "You're
going to give me a little extra,
right?" all the while with his
hand on my butt, squeezing. I
really didn't know how to react,
so I gave him extra Twizzlers.

I'm really not sure where
Dani was during the day while we
were at school. I think my
mother had a job, although I'm
not sure where. My mother's
aunt, our great aunt, watched us
for a short time, so she must
have watched Dani too, maybe.
My mother's aunt was actually
younger than her by a few years,
which always confused me when I
was young. My great aunt was
nice. She had kids that were
close to our ages, two boys, and
they were nice boys. My great
aunt had a live-in boyfriend,
and I could almost swear didn't
speak English. I know he was
speaking English, but something
about the way he talked,

insanely fast, or something
equally incomprehensible
prevented me from understanding
a single word that came out of
his mouth. It was very odd to
me. I would hear him have
conversations with adults, and
they seemed to be able to carry
on a conversation with him.
They may have just pretended to
understand to be polite, but
they appeared to understand. I
would watch his mouth, and try
so hard to understand his words,
but it was impossible.

Even with my great aunt,
our two nice second cousins, and
the non-comprehendible live-in
boyfriend, we did not like going
over there. My great aunt also
had a daughter, one which I will
just call "Scary," that was a
few years older than my brother.
She was a rather large, very
loud girl, and I remember a
whole lot of teeth. I don't
really know how to explain what
I mean by that, "a whole lot of
teeth," except they were very
crowded, and I swear she had

more than she was supposed to
have, like multiple rows of
teeth. She actually was quite
scary, and she wasn't very nice
to Scarlett or her brothers.
I'm pretty sure she sexually
abused Gerald during this time,
as well. I never knew any
details, other than that
something happened. "Scary" was
very scary.

     She was, however, nice to
me and I'm not quite sure why.
She was still scary, even in her
niceness. She always liked to
fix my hair and do my makeup,
but while applying my makeup she
would also throw in subtle
insults, telling me I could
never wear model makeup because
my eyes were too small. I
remember that really upset me
because I wanted to be a model,
and I believed her. What did I
know? I was only in third
grade. I remember listening to
Debbie Gibson and Madonna,
dancing with Scary with over-
teased hair and dark green
eyeshadow up to my eyebrows. I

think she liked having someone to talk to. She would tell me about her love life, her crushes, her social life, her personal experiences, most of which I wish she would have kept to herself.

One particular experience she shared with me I wish I could forget. It involved a certain crush she had at the time. It must have been in the fall because Scary was going on a hayride with this current crush. She thought it would be a good idea to cut his name in her jeans. It was the style in the 80s to have ripped or intentionally cut, frosted or bleached jeans, so that in itself wasn't that odd. But Scary was a big girl. The intentional cuts gave way to her fat every time she sat down, so this crush's name was oozing out of these intentional cuts and his name was spelled out in her fat. As I said before, Scary was scary, even in her niceness.

When my stepfather got out
of prison, I vaguely remember
him living in a halfway house.
I'm really not even sure how
long he was in prison, but at
some point, he was living with
us again. I'm not sure why I
brought it up to my mother, but
I really did not like my
stepfather. I did not like him
at all. I don't know if there
was a specific event that scared
me, or if it was just the fact
that he was back from prison, or
if it was just the evilness that
radiated off of him, but I
remember sitting in the back
yard with my mother and begging
her not to let him live with us.
I thought I was so convincing.
My mother cried, and she nodded
in agreement. In my nine or
ten-year-old mind I actually
thought he wasn't going to live
with us anymore. I thought I
had convinced her he was bad for
our family. Of course, he
continued to live with us.

14 ~ Galewood
Kettering, Ohio

With my stepfather back in the picture, we were able to move back to Kettering. We moved into a nice house in a nicer neighborhood. This was during the middle of my third-grade year, sometime after Valentine's Day. We were able to go back to Tara Elementary, which was what we were used to. My stepfather started driving a semi-truck, which was his profession before he met my mother, so he was gone a lot. We didn't care one bit, but maybe my mother did. I'm really not sure.

My mother seemed to be thriving, and life seemed to be going in a positive direction. My mother was back in college and doing her art. I haven't talked about my mother's art yet. My mother was an art student at Shawnee State College when we were very young. I remember visiting the college and being fascinated by a giant sculpture of E.T. in the hallway whose heart really glowed red. My mother was the most amazing artist I've ever known. She had this amazing talent, or rather a rare gift. She was a painter, a sculpture, and the best sketch artist I have ever seen. She has won multiple awards and has even sold a few portraits.

My mother was thriving or at least trying to thrive. We had a nice house in a nice neighborhood. She had her garden again. She had her art studio. She had her husband, not in prison. Around this time my stepfather hurt his back and was no longer able to work, so he was home all the time. He still had his occasional blowups for reasons that never made much sense to me, but things were mostly calm.

One blowup specifically reinforced my fear of my

stepfather, not that it ever went away. We were told to put our clean laundry away and my brother dropped a pair of underwear as he was walking down the hallway. I really don't think he even knew he dropped them, or maybe his plan was to lay the rest of his laundry down, then come back to pick up that dropped pair of underwear as he would be less likely to drop the other clothes he was carrying. Who knows what he was thinking, but it sure set Stuart off? A reasonable person would likely say, "Hey, you dropped something." My brother, not the type of person to drop underwear on the floor and just leave them, could have explained rationally, "Oh, I didn't realize I dropped them," or scenario two, "I need to put these down first, so I won't drop everything else." My stepfather was never one to be rational though. That single pair of underwear on the floor angered him so terribly that he chased my brother down the hallway and grabbed him by the hair on the top of his head and threw him down. I really don't remember anything that happened after that, but I know I was scared to drop any of my laundry as I walked down the hallway. I am pretty sure I saw my stepfather shove my mother down in the hallway once. I have no idea why, and it was just that once. I still thought he had the evilest eyes I'd ever seen on a human being, but if he wasn't glaring at me it was okay. For the most part, things were pretty good or looked good to an outsider looking in.

If you were an insider and you were paying attention at all you would have seen the Invisible Monster was rearing its ugly head, only this time the monster was not invisible. My brother had become the monster, and his prey had become more abundant and more vulnerable. This vulnerability allowed the monster to become more dangerous. If you were an insider and you were paying attention you might find it odd and inappropriate for a 12-year-old boy to take a bath with his sister who is only two. Surely this wasn't normal behavior. Why was it not viewed as a problem when Gerald would want to have Dani sleep in his bed with him?

Around this time Dani started experiencing what I know now as telltale signs of sexual abuse. She would do this thing we called "exercising," and we thought it was hilarious. She looked funny when she was "exercising." I didn't know what she was doing or why she was doing this, but if we would catch her, she would get extremely embarrassed. That just gave us more of a reason to laugh. I didn't understand at the time, but the sad truth is she was actually sexually stimulating herself. She was very aware of sexual sensation at the age of two, and she liked it.

There were multiple
occasions where we were playing
"house," or something
comparable, and Dani would
pretend she was married to one
of her stuffed animals, a mouse
named Fievel Mousekewits, a
character from the movie, "An
American Tail." Fievel was
about the same size as Dani, and
he had removable pants. Dani
would take Fievel up on the top
bunk of the bunk beds and take
off his pants. I really didn't
know what she was doing up
there. I only know that she
didn't want us to see, and if
she saw us watching her, she
would get really upset. That
should have been a giant, red,
extremely visible flag flying
full staff to any responsible,
loving parent, or to at least
anyone who bothered to see that
giant red flag. I am burdened
with the guilt of not
recognizing, or at least not
understanding, there was a
problem. I should have been

protecting Dani from the Invisible Monster.

So many instances were mentioned during this time, but they were only mentioned once and then never mentioned again. Ashley told me she woke up in the middle of the night with my brother trying to put his hand down the front of her pants. For whatever reason, she hadn't put on pajamas. She was still wearing the jeans that she had worn that day, which was actually lucky for her. Gerald had to unzip her jeans before he could put his hand down her pants. Her jeans were much more difficult than pajamas to get down so, of course, she woke up in the process. She told him to go away, and he did. I'm not sure if I was the only one she told, and sadly I don't even remember my reaction when she told me of this traumatic event.

I don't remember any details, or how I even know this, but a little girl that we

spent a lot of time with was
also a victim of my brother.
This was the same little girl
that was bitten by our dog,
Loki, resulting in him being put
to sleep. She was younger,
maybe a year or two younger than
my younger sister, but older
than my baby sister. Another
childhood friend, a young boy,
told me after spending the night
with us that he woke up to my
brother fondling his penis.
This was new, a boy had never
told me this before. I remember
thinking it was weird that he
did this to boys too. I'm not
sure if he told his mom, my
mother's friend, but he never
came over again. Actually,
other than one occasion when we
were teenagers, I never saw him
again after that.

Another instance that was
probably more damaging, my
mother woke up to my brother
feeling her boobs. I don't know
anything else beyond that, only
that that's what she woke up to.
I don't know how she reacted, if

she was angry, if she was sad, if she was confused, if she enjoyed it. I just remember hearing about it that one time and never again. When I say this instance was probably more damaging, I feel this was probably more damaging to my brother. Why didn't she react appropriately? He needed help, severely, and my mother preferred to pretend there wasn't a problem, or my mother was part of the problem. The Invisible Monster rears its ugly head. Did my mother create this monster?

We finished out the school year at Tara Elementary, but for whatever reason, the school zoning changed over the summer. When school started in the fall, we went to Indian Riffle Elementary. This was the school that Ashley went to, so she, my sister, and I were all in the same elementary school for the first time. I was in fourth grade, Ashley was in third, and Scarlett was held back and was repeating first grade, not because of her academics but more her maturity level. I know now it had nothing to with her maturity level but her life exposure, neglect, and abuse. She had so much internal chaotic confusion in a big, jumbled mess in her six-year-old mind, that she had no way of understanding. It is painfully obvious to me that this was the true cause of her being held back a year. If someone was paying attention my sister could have been protected better and received the help she needed.

It was rather odd going to school with Ashley since we never had before. Kettering has multiple elementary schools that all feed into one large middle school (referred to as junior high at the time), and one large high school. Even though we were in Kettering schools in the past this was our first shared school experience with her.

Our only common past experiences were confined to Ashley's weekend visits, and she and I got along great. She was extremely mean to Scarlett, although I never knew why. The only thing I could rationalize was that she was nice to me because I was older and mean to her because she was younger, which really doesn't seem very rational, but that's what I thought. My sister and I were always very close, whether Ashley was there or not, but we also fought like you wouldn't believe.

Now back to the oddness of attending the same elementary school as Ashley. I would see her during recess sometimes and she behaved like the biggest snob ever. She acted as if she didn't know me, or she and her snobby, already established friends would say mean things to me, although I don't remember any specifics. Then Friday evening would roll around and she and I would be best friends for the weekend, and she would be a snob to Scarlett. Actually, the exact same behavior I experienced during the week at school from Ashely was the same behavior Scarlett experienced on the weekends.

I liked going to Indian Riffle Elementary School. I made new friends, and I still had other friends that were re-zoned like us. I had a very nice, young teacher named Mr. Page. I think it was his first year teaching, so he was full of energy and so much fun. My grandmother told me she thought he was cute, but I didn't see it. We studied Ohio history that year and I loved it. Mr. Page dressed up as an American Indian and did a whole big skit. He tried to get me to be involved in the skit because of my teepee history, but I was way too shy at the time. He also taught us to play "stiff as a board, light as a feather," right there in the middle of the classroom floor.

This was the year a teacher was chosen to go to space with a group of astronauts. It was all over the news because this was huge. Never had a teacher been chosen to be involved in such an experience. Everyone made such a big deal about it at school, understandably so. This was before televisions were in every classroom, so we all crammed into the library to watch the space shuttle take off. How exciting it was as we all waited in anticipation for the space shuttle to take off. There was complete silence in the library as we watched in amazement and excitement as the space shuttle was launched. Early on during the liftoff, there was once again complete silence in the library, only this time it was shock and horror. The space shuttle exploded shortly after it had taken off as the whole world watched. The explosion killed everyone on the space shuttle instantly, the teacher included. The television was

shut off immediately and we went
back to class. I really don't
think anyone in my fourth-grade
class really understood what we
had just witnessed, or at least
I didn't.

I have so many more
insignificant memories while we
lived in this house. I remember
Gerald running bathwater and
falling asleep, flooding the
entire bathroom, which soaked
the carpet all the way down the
hall. I remember a teenage boy
who lived next door, I think,
but I don't remember ever seeing
him. I just remember very loud
Metallica, or Pantera, or
whatever, coming from what I
assumed was his bedroom. I
don't remember ever minding,
just one of those things I
remember. My mother's sister
and her ex-husband had their
wedding reception at our house,
and I remember my ex-uncle
asking my mother to use her
bedroom for a quickie.

I remember Gerald and I washing dishes together and singing. I even remember one of the songs we would sing. I'm not sure if my brother made it up, or where he learned it, but I sure do remember it, and it was definitely insignificant.

"Mr. Alligator was pulling some weeds. Pulling 'til his arms were beat. He said I know what I need now. I know what I'd like. I feel like having something to eat. I'm going to go on home now and do it right away. You know I can't put it off 'til later. It just seems like the right thing to do today. I'm going to raid that refrigerator. I'm going to raid that refrigerator."

15 ~ Not Yet, I Have Big Plans For You

Insignificant situations as a child are not always so insignificant when you're an adult looking back. Like waking up in the middle of the night to a bunch of flashing lights, then wandering out into the living room to look out the window. What I saw was a car smashed into a tree in our front yard, pretty close and on the exact course, to my bedroom where I was sleeping moments ago. I saw an ambulance, fire truck, and I'm sure police cars, but mainly I just remember red flashing lights. I got up, saw this scene out the window, and went back to bed without giving the situation a second thought.

As an adult looking back this is actually pretty horrifying. A speeding car being driven by a young drunk man crashed into the tree just feet from our bedroom. The car was on a direct course to the bedroom Scarlett, Dani, and I shared, with our bunk beds against the outer wall, just feet from the tree that saved our lives. Do I call that luck? Or was that God's protective hand guarding his children? The Universe knew we weren't done yet, there were much bigger things to come.

I had a similar experience a few years later while waiting to cross the street at a crosswalk in Dayton. After pushing the button for the crosswalk, as I was standing on the corner, I watched in horror, unable to move, as a large truck drove up onto the sidewalk. It went up on the sidewalk, back onto the road, then once again onto the sidewalk, smashing into a pole a few feet in front of me. It happened so fast! That pole saved my life. Even if I didn't know yet, God had very, very big plans for me.

We had friends a few houses down that we played with all the time, or rather Scarlett and I, and sometimes Ashely, played with them all the time. I brought Dani down to their house some, but she was still pretty small then. We were very good friends with them. I was pretty close with the oldest of the boys who was one year older than me. I know now he was gay; he was the one I got along with the best. This would prove to be a lifelong trend of mine, being close friends with gay men. I understand the psychology behind that trend now, gay men are "safe" men in my subconscious mind. He introduced me to Tiffany, an 80s singer that was popular at the time, and he taught me to crochet.

The next boy was a year younger than me and had the biggest crush on me, and he was not shy about it one bit. It was very annoyingly clear he had a crush on me. He would never leave me alone, always chasing me and saying inappropriate things. I still played with him, but he got on my nerves. The youngest was the only girl. She may have been around the same age as Scarlett. We loved her too. She was so sweet and pretty, and she was so much fun to play with. I'm pretty sure they had an older brother, too, but he was older and didn't play with us.

Despite everything we were still happy kids, at least that is how I remember it. We had a nice swing set in the backyard. We had friends to play with that lived very close. I remember burying a time capsule with my friends in the backyard of that Galewood house. I wonder if it's still there. During this time, we weren't spending much time in bars. My mother was doing well. She was back in art school. She had an art studio set up and was creating masterpieces again. She had a nice garden in the back yard. I'm not sure if she was working at this time, or just focusing on school. Stuart must have had Worker's Comp or something because we were able to maintain that house for about a year and a half.

On the rare occasion my mother would go out she would get a sitter like Scary with all the teeth. Scary was never a good sitter at all. She would invite drunk teenage boys to our house while she was supposed to be watching us. Once, there were a small group of these drunk teenage boys, one of which was trying to pick a fight with Gerald because he wouldn't come out of his room. Another fell in the hallway and busted a hole in the wall. The third of this little group of drunk teenage boys was standing in our kitchen with his pants and underwear down around his ankles, completely exposed. By this time Dani was maybe four years old and, of course, saw all of this. She pointed to his fully exposed penis, and said, "Look, a pee-pee!" Scary thought it was hilarious. She leaned up against the fully exposed penis to block Dani's view, all the while laughing. Maybe we would have been better off going to the bar.

Even though we weren't spending too much time in bars then I do remember spending an occasional evening in the upstairs loft of a gay bar that was owned by my mother's cousin and his husband, Gary. Their marriage turned one of my best friends at the time into my cousin. Gary's sister was one of my mother's best drinking friends, and she had a daughter named Joy. My mother was always drinking with her mother, so by proxy, Joy and I were best friends. We decide the best way to describe our relationship was cousins because the actual description was a little confusing. I'm not really sure what you call your mom's male cousin's husband's niece.

We had a pretty big social circle with my mother and her drinking friends. I remember spending a lot of time with Bonnie, who was Dani's God Mother, whatever that means. She had a daughter who was a year older than me. We were good friends too. We spent so much time at Bonnie's house, and we loved it. There were always different adults at Bonnie's within that group of drinking friends, and maybe some extra kids on occasion. The adults were always drinking, and there were always joints and bongs being passed around with no regard for the children in the room. I'm sure I have had many contact buzzes over the years. Weed was never hidden from us, therefore we never thought of it as a big deal.

The later it would get, the louder the adults would get. My mother and Bonnie, and whoever else was there at the time, would turn Janis Joplin up so loud. They would sing and dance late into the night, and they would have so much fun. I'll admit, it was fun to watch at times, and quite often we would join in on the late-night dance party, but other times I just wanted to go home and go to sleep. Bonnie was in the picture for years. I'm not sure when she came into the picture, but it was definitely a long-term relationship, or maybe it just seemed that way when I was younger. We really loved her. She seemed to have it all together, way more than my mother did. She was nice to us, and she sure loved Dani.

16 ~ Wilkes, West Virginia (somewhere)

My father was still going to NA meetings regularly. He moved in with one of his friends from those meetings, who lived in Wilkes, West Virginia. This is where our West Virginia roots started. His friend had been burned in a fire and was covered from head to toe with burn scars. Even his fingers were drawn up from scar tissue. His nose was burnt down to the cartilage. Needless (and shallow) to say, we were scared to death of him. He had a really big, nice house and appeared to be quite wealthy. I'm sure he got a huge settlement because his accident was a work-related injury, a factory fire if I remember correctly. I think his drug addiction was also a result of his accident. He later died of an overdose. Around this same time my father started dating

someone by the name of Renee,
who was from also from NA. I
loved Renee!

   We would occasionally visit
our father, although I'm not
sure how frequently. I had very
bad separation anxiety whenever
I was with my father. This
anxiety was not for my mother at
all, but for my baby sister,
Dani. After returning from a
visit with my father once I
remember I was so happy to be
home. I busted through the door
with my arms out in anticipation
of a great big hug. I know my
mother thought this excitement
was for her, so she had her arms
outstretched in the same
anticipation. But rather than
running to my mother's
outstretched arms I dropped to
my knees and wrapped my arms
tightly around Dani. I never
wanted to let her go. I know
that hurt my mother's feelings,
but Dani was who I longed for.
I didn't care.

My mother and Stuart started having problems around this time, although I really don't remember much fighting or anything. I just remember Stuart was no longer there. I never asked why, nor did I really care. I knew my mother was upset, but Stuart was no good for us and I knew that. My brother had decided to go live with our father around this time, as well, and I don't remember having any feelings about that whatsoever. He was just gone, and I was okay with that. So now it was only my mother, Scarlett, Dani, and myself, and I was so sure we were all better for it.

17 ~ Van Buren Apartments # 1
Kettering, Ohio

I was able to finish fourth grade at Indian Riffle Elementary, but once school was out, we moved to a very small two-bedroom apartment. This apartment was still in Kettering, but we were back in Tara School District. Since it was summertime Scarlett was with our father. When given a choice I typically chose to stay in Ohio with Dani. We liked it there. It was relatively calm during this time. My mother had a new job doing landscaping, which she really enjoyed. We were doing okay.

I really don't remember seeing much of Stuart during this time. I'm not sure where he was, he just wasn't in the picture. He did come to our apartment once and my mother told me not to let him in. It was so horribly awkward. I

could see him through the
window, and I could hear his
voice begging me to open the
door. My mother was inside
instructing me not to open the
door. I didn't open the door,
of course, but it was a scary
situation, nonetheless. Stuart
slid cash under the door and
told me to give it to my mother,
which he said was his whole
reason for being there. I know
he was there another time,
although I never saw him. I
just heard him and my mother in
the living room having sex on
the couch late one night.

Scary was not watching us
anymore. We now had a new
sitter, Melanie, for the summer.
She was the daughter of another
of my mother's drunk friends.
This drunken friend later died
of an overdose, as well. We
really liked Melanie, but I am
pretty sure my mother didn't pay
her properly. Plus, my mother
never came straight home after
work. She usually ended up at
Hank's Pub, which was

conveniently right next door to her new job. She would stumble in late, sometimes we were awake, sometimes we were not. I have no idea if Melanie stayed the night, or how she got home, or any other detail regarding the situation.

I woke up one of the nights my mother didn't come home until after I was asleep to use the bathroom, and I heard my mother having sex…again. I knew what I was hearing. It's not like I had never heard my mother having sex before. Recently I even overheard her in the living room having sex with Stuart on the couch. At least that time I was able to stay in my room, but this time I really had to use the bathroom. I didn't have a choice. I had to get up. At least the sex sounds were coming from my mother's waterbed, so I knew she was in her bedroom. I thought maybe she and Stuart were possibly getting back together, especially since I had heard them having sex recently.

My mother must have heard me get
up because she started crying.
I wasn't sure why she was crying
until I heard the voice that
followed, and it was definitely
not Stuart. It was Stuart's
best friend, also named Stewart,
but spelled differently. I just
went back to bed.

18 ~ Van Buren Apartments #2
Kettering, Ohio

My mother met her new boyfriend at the landscaping company she was working for. He seemed nice enough and they decided to move in together. Summer was over so Scarlett was back, and my mother's new boyfriend had a daughter that would visit on weekends. That small, two-bedroom apartment just wouldn't work anymore. We moved to a townhouse within the same apartment complex so we would have more room. I was starting fifth grade; Scarlett was starting second. We were once again at Tara Elementary. Life seemed to be moving in a positive direction again, but it was short-lived as usual.

My mother and her boyfriend argued often. In relationships arguments are normal, but these arguments didn't seem normal. I would frequently hear them arguing from their bedroom when I was trying to sleep, arguments I wish I could un-hear. On more occasions than I care to remember I would hear them arguing about sex, and it absolutely disgusted me. I can still hear her screaming at him because he would scratch and cut her "every time he would finger her." And if the words alone weren't enough, the imagery is unimaginable. You see, he was one of those people who didn't care too much about hygiene and he never cut his fingernails (or brushed his teeth for that matter). His fingernails were incredibly long and black. Not just dingy and dirty, they were black. He was a landscaper, who didn't wear gloves while at work, who didn't cut his fingernails. So, this argument I overheard, knowing now what my mother actually meant, and remembering the condition of her boyfriend's fingernails, I would like nothing more than to un-hear this argument.

My mother's boyfriend eventually left, and my mother couldn't afford the townhouse on her own. She didn't have a job anymore since she was working with her boyfriend. I know she was depressed and overly stressed. I get it, I really do. But my mother also gained her freedom. Finally, finally, as if this were the day she had been waiting for since the day she had children, she no longer felt we needed a sitter. She didn't have to find and pay someone to watch us, nor did she have to take us to the bar with her, and Hank's Pub was definitely where she was spending her time these days.

I have absolutely no memory of my mother during this time. I'm sure she had to be there at least part of the time, but if she was, I know she wasn't available. Like the time one of my baby molars was so rotten that it just crumbled to pieces leaving a small remnant of a rotten tooth under the surface.

I ended up with an odd puss-
filled blister on the surface of
my gums, right next to that
embedded piece of rotten tooth.
I now know it was an abscess.
It was very painful, but my
mother was never around, nor
seemed to care enough about our
well-being, so I didn't even
bother telling her about it. I
just got some type of sharp
utensil, maybe a needle or a
small knife, and dug down into
my gums until I was able to pry
that piece of rotten tooth out,
causing the abscess to burst in
the process. I had instant
relief with or without my
mother's assistance, and I
simultaneously became obsessed
with having healthy teeth.

19 ~ West Virginia (somewhere)

I have no memory of how I became aware of this new situation, or rather an old situation where someone was finally paying attention, but there was finally some blowback to my brother's behavior. My father married the lady he had been dating from NA, Renee. So, when Gerald moved with our father, he also moved with Renee and her son. Shortly after he got there my stepmother woke up in the middle of the night finding Gerald fondling her boobs. Obviously, she freaked out because this was not normal behavior. Renee wanted to take action immediately. Finally, someone was paying attention!

I'm not exactly sure how things played out from that point, but I think Gerald was taken to Highland Hospital, which was a mental health facility in Charleston, West

Virginia. From there he was placed in a foster home and stayed there for quite a while, but I'm not sure how long.

My father made sure that my mother was aware of the situation, but she only blamed him. She said the things he was saying were not true, even though my mother woke to Gerald fondling her boobs a few years prior. She said Gerald wouldn't do that. She blamed Scary because she molested Gerald. If anything did happen at all that's where it came from, but she didn't believe that it happened at all. My mother either pulled her blinders back over her eyes that day, or maybe she was upset because the secret was out. Whatever her reasoning was she didn't act appropriately, which raises that nagging question forever in the back of my brain. Is my mother the Invisible Monster?

My father picked Scarlett and me up for a visit during

this time and decided we should have counseling because of Gerald. This was my first experience with counseling, and it did not go over well at all. First of all, she made sure to tell me that the things Gerald did were not my fault. No fucking duh, it was not my fault. It was Gerald's fault, and that Invisible Monster who ruined him as a small child, but for damn sure it wasn't my fault. Strike one with this counselor.

Strike two was when she was using big words, words I don't remember today, but words that I was fully aware of their meaning at the time. She was using these big words to describe what was going on with Gerald. As she was using these big words, she felt the need to define them and then ask me if I knew what these words meant. Of course, I knew the meaning of these words and I felt like she talking to me like I was stupid. I was not stupid, and I could definitely

understand her big words.
Strike two, I decided I didn't
like counseling.

20 ~ Grandparents' House #1
Kettering, Ohio

We moved in with my grandparents, my mother's parents, but I don't remember exactly when. At the time I didn't know why, but I'm sure it was because we were evicted. Scarlett, Dani, and I all shared a bedroom, and my mother had a bedroom to herself. My mother must have been there occasionally because her room smelled like beer and cigarettes, but I really don't remember her being there at all. The smell of beer was not that of actual beer in the room, but of the "alcoholic" odor seeping from her pores.

My grandparents did live within walking distance to Hank's Pub, so I would say that is where my mother spent most of her time. On one occasion we must have been at the bar with her because I remember the walk

back to my grandparents' house.
On our walk back my mother
tripped and fell on the ground.
We just assumed she had too much
to drink, and we thought it was
hilarious. Laughing at her may
not have been the appropriate
response as she struggled to get
up, but that's what we did. She
wasn't hurt, just drunk, and she
sure got mad at us for laughing.

It's funny, I really don't
remember my grandparents much
during that time either. Of
course, they had to be there, I
just don't really remember them,
but what I do remember was
usually irritation with us for
being there. Our room was too
messy, our pet hamsters were
stinky, we were too loud, etc.
I don't fault them for their
irritation either. My mother
wasn't there, which is not what
they expected, I'm sure. They
were helping their daughter,
they thought.

The small bedroom Scarlett,
Dani, and I shared had one

single-size bed and a small foldable cot. Since I was the oldest I wanted the cot so I wouldn't have to share a bed, Scarlett and Dani were to share the single bed. But every night Dani slept on the tiny little cot with me. She always liked to sleep in my arms, and I liked it too. I would sing to her, and hold her, and comfort her, and love her. Dani was my baby. Since Dani always slept with me, I'm not sure why I chose the smaller cot, which was situated against the common wall between my grandparents' room and the room we were sharing. In our cuddles on that tiny little cot, we would bump the wall, on occasion, and my grandmother would come in yelling. She couldn't understand why two of us were cramming in that little cot, making all that noise, when there was a bigger bed we could share. I couldn't give her an answer because I didn't know the answer at that time. Now, I understand. During the daytime hours, I was the oldest and it

made sense to sleep alone, and
that was always my plan. But
then during the nighttime hours,
our vulnerable hours, I had to
keep Dani in my arms to know she
was safe.

Relatively close to the end
of that school year, my fifth-
grade year, my mother
disappeared. Before, when I
said my mother was never there.
I'm pretty sure she did come
home every evening, but very
late. If I were to guess I
would have to say she probably
would stumble in around 3:00
when the bar closed, but I never
really knew for sure. But this
time was different, she didn't
come home for three days. I
don't remember knowing she
hadn't come home, but I must
have. I just didn't care. We
didn't see her much then anyway.
When my mother finally did come
home, she told my grandparents
she was arrested for a DUI, and
when she was released, she was
too ashamed to come home. My
grandparents definitely did not

want us there after that. Scarlett and I were sent to West Virginia with our father and were unable to finish the school year. Technically, I never finished 5th grade.

Dani's father was her more responsible parent at that time, or rather his new girlfriend was more responsible, so Dani went to live with them. More responsible does not mean responsible by normal standards, but it was the better choice. Stuart and his new girlfriend were cocaine addicts or something. Stuart was driving a semi-truck, again, so Dani was alone with his girlfriend most of the time. Despite her habits/addictions she sure loved Dani, and Dani knew it. Stuart's girlfriend was very focused and had a lot of energy, which was spent purely on taking care of Dani. I know now all that "energy" was from cocaine, but I didn't care as long as my baby sister was being taken care of. I felt comfortable with

Stuart's new girlfriend caring for Dani when I was in West Virginia. I knew she was relatively safe, but that did not change the fact that I missed Dani more than I could ever describe. I brought two drawings that she had given me before I left. One, just colorful scribbles, and the other was a basic stick figure with the arms coming out of the sides of the head, with my name written out in Dani's four-year-old handwriting. She had given them to me, and I treasured them, I still treasure them. I taped the drawings above the bed where I slept, and I would lay there for hours staring at them. I missed my baby so much! I would kiss my hand, then place that kiss on those drawings every night as I would say, "I love you, Dani." My heart physically hurt from missing her so much, but I was just a kid. What could I do about anything?

Gerald still lived in a foster home, maybe, I just know

he wasn't there. That was an interesting summer for sure. In Ohio, at home, I was used to my mother not being home. She decided I was old enough to care for two younger siblings while she was gone. I was a very responsible little girl, yet my father decided Scarlett and I needed a babysitter, which did not go over very well. I think the lady that watched us was a friend of my stepmother's, and she had the evilest little boy. He hit Scarlett in the head with a hammer once, on purpose! After that things became very difficult.

My father then decided we would do better in daycare. Are you serious? I was taking care of my little sisters at home, doing everything, without the assistance of an adult. Daycare! Now, that one really did not go over well. We only lasted a few days before we were kicked out. There was one little girl who cried from the time she was dropped off in the morning until the time she was picked up in the evening. I tried to console and comfort her was told not to. They said she cried every day, and I was to leave her alone and let her cry. Not a very good first impression. She was a little girl and she just wanted her mom, I got it. I was used to cuddling and comforting Dani when she was upset and I knew I could make that little girl feel better, but the daycare workers wouldn't let me.

Scarlett and I did not want to be there, and we made sure everyone knew it. We lead the entire daycare in the rebellious act of pounding a beat on the lunch table while chanting the lyrics, "We will, we will, rock you." I don't know what prompted us to do this, as it was definitely out of character for us both. We were usually good kids, but not that day. The daycare workers were furious, yelling at us to stop, which only encouraged us to pound and chant louder all the while laughing hysterically. I'm pretty sure we weren't allowed to come back after that. Oh well.

Eventually, we landed at the YMCA Day Camp, which we loved. This atmosphere was structured and supervised, yet fun and exciting. We got to go swimming most days, and we took really fun field trips every week. Scarlett and I were very popular there. That's also probably around the same time I started getting a lot of attention from boys, or at least attention I didn't mind getting. That was the summer I had my first boyfriend, but the kind of boyfriend you only talk to through other people and shyly smile at each other from across the camp. Scarlett and I did have a lot of fun there. We went to Carter Caves in Kentucky for an overnight camping trip and got to tour the caves. We toured a coal mine somewhere in West Virginia, went to a glass factory, a television station, a minor league baseball game, and countless other exciting field trips. We went swimming at FMC Pool, or the wave pool, every day that was a non-field trip day. We were able to experience so much because we were there.

I really loved all the attention I was getting from my stepmother, Renee. She only had a son, so she enjoyed doting over two little girls. We were at a store once and a pair of black, leather, Roman style sandals caught my eye, and she bought them for me. I know that doesn't seem like much, but I wasn't used to getting new things. My grandmother occasional bought us clothes, but most everything we owned were hand-me-downs. Renee bought me those sandals simply because she knew I wanted them. I wore them to camp the next day and they were stolen while we were at the wave pool, and I was crushed, but that's not the point. The point is Renee loved me. She bought me my first bra, she permed my hair, and she was so much fun. We even got to see Run-DMC in concert that summer! And she was the first adult that ever seemed to notice, or care, there was an Invisible Monster lurking in the dark. Renee later died of a drug overdose, but it was long after her and my father divorced.

I was having fun at camp, and Renee's motherly love was something I had never experienced before, but it was not enough. I still kissed my hand and placed the kisses on the pictures Dani had drawn for me, saying, "I love you, Dani," every single night with tears in my eyes. I just wanted to be home so I could be with Dani. The longing was excruciating.

21 ~ Dayton, Ohio (some guy's floor)

We ended up back with my mother at some point. The plan was, I assume, to get settled before school started. The situation we were in was nothing but settling, and we were definitely not settled before school started. We spent the first few weeks of school going to the same Kettering school we were taken out of early the prior school year when my mother disappeared. I was very uncomfortable with all the kids asking me where I went last year when I disappeared. I mean, what do you say? "My mom was in jail and I had to go to my dad's." This is not something you want to tell your friends at school. It didn't matter though; we were only there a few weeks before we started back in Dayton Public Schools.

While Scarlett and I were in West Virginia my mother had gotten back together with her boyfriend, Frank, the same boyfriend that had previously left her, which ultimately led to us living with my grandparents. My mother and her boyfriend were living with some guy, and maybe some kids. Dani was still staying primarily with her father and his girlfriend, but at least I was able to see her.

I really don't remember that time well, but Scarlett and I were sleeping on the nasty brown carpet on the floor of my mother and her boyfriend's bedroom. I vaguely remember drunk people, and maybe a dog that had puppies chained up out back, and the house was a typical Dayton, old, junked up, 100 plus year-old house with no air conditioning and dirty carpet. I don't think we lived here for very long.

22 ~ Oak Street, Dayton Ohio (Sixth Grade)

We moved to our own house in Dayton right after I started sixth grade. I will have to say thus far this was the coolest house I've ever lived in, but then again, anything would seem nice compared to that nasty brown carpet we were sleeping on in the floor of my mother's bedroom. The house was very old and wasn't kept up as it should have been. It was turned into a duplex somewhere along the way. I loved that house.

First of all, the house was way bigger than anything we had ever lived in, even as a duplex. The detail was amazing. The house was built in the 1890s and it was definitely an impressive home in its day. I was never on the other side of the duplex, but I would imagine the layout was similar. The only difference was it didn't have a second bathroom downstairs as we did. The woodwork was beautiful. There were panel doors that slid into the walls to separate the front parlor from the living room. There was a wooden staircase with a big, thick, wooden banister. The wood flooring was in rough shape, but all original. There was floor to ceiling built-in cabinets in the dining room, all original and functional. The light switches were even original, the old-fashioned two button style, (top button to turn the lights on, bottom button to turn the lights off) and yes, the lights were sconces on the wall and not overhead lights. There was even a claw-foot bathtub in the upstairs bathroom.

There were three bedrooms on the second floor, which meant I got to have my own room. Dani slept with me when she was there, though, even though she and Scarlett technically shared a room. This house was so large

that it had a full basement with
two cellars we referred to as
dungeons (we used to hold
seances in them), as well as a
full, finished attic with its
own hidden stairway inside one
of the closets. As big and as
beautiful as this house was, it
was still very, very run down
and had many flaws.

We actually thought the
attic was haunted, but not in a
bad way. We found an old-
fashioned hospital bed in the
attic when we first moved in.
It was so old that it had a
handle that had to be manually
cranked in order to raise and
lower the bed. The old mattress
was still on the bed with a
deep, permanent body imprint.
It gave the impression that
someone had laid there, tucked
away in the attic, for a very
long time, maybe even died
there. My mother threw away the
mattress because it felt eerie
for it to be there, but there
was no way to get the bed out.
I swear we heard that bed

cranking up and creaking at night. It could have been just some random noises that old houses like that make, but we were convinced it was coming from the attic and we definitely thought it was a ghost. We didn't feel scared or threatened though. It was just a presence that we were more than happy to share our space with.

I really loved that house, as run down as it was, and with the ghost in the attic, this house would be my home for three years. This was the longest I had ever lived in one location to this point, although the location was less than ideal. We were again in the Dayton Public School system, and the conveniently located bar at this end of the street would become my mother's new hangout. Although this location wasn't the worst part of Dayton, I wouldn't call it good by any means.

I just started sixth grade and Scarlett was in third grade. Again, the whole drawing names from a hat scenario that would determine which Dayton Public School we would attend. It was decided that Scarlett and I would attend Carlson Elementary School smack dab in the middle of a ghetto on the other side of Dayton. We had over an hour bus ride every morning and every afternoon to attend this school, even though there were two elementary schools within walking distance to our house. At least they kept Scarlett and me together this time, and we did have a lot of fun on the bus. We both did okay at this school for the most part. I was always a good student and Scarlett was doing much better after a semi-rough start.

Scarlett had somewhat of a traumatic experience on our first day at Carlson Elementary though. My grandmother had recently taken Scarlett to get her hair cut by the same stylist that cut her hair. I'm not sure if Scarlett wanted her hair cut that short, or it was my grandmother's decision to have it cut similar to hers. Poor Scarlett came out looking like a little boy. On the first day of school, Scarlett had to use the restroom. Since we were new, we went into the office to ask for directions. We followed the directions given to us by the office personnel and ended up at the boys' bathroom, not the girls'. This actually happened on more than one occasion. She was given the key to the boys' bathroom at the library, as well. Poor Scarlett! She has had long, or semi-long, hair since.

For the most part, I liked going to school there. I had good friends, my teacher was awesome and pregnant, and I was able to be at the same school as Scarlett. I thrived there, at least while at school. I was chosen to be in The Young Author's Club. I made good grades, except in handwriting. I had a lot of friends. I met one of my soon-to-be best friends there, India. To this day she still has a special place in my heart. I was getting a lot of attention from the boys, which I enjoyed. One exception was when a boy passed me a note in class. I opened it and I was shocked. It was a drawing of a guy with a big, cartoonish penis. I was more than shocked, I was disgusted! Dayton Public Schools were way different than the "fancy" Kettering schools we were used to.

The only negative experience I had at this school was initiated by me being in the Young Authors' Club, although indirectly. On one of our special field trips, Young Authors only, we were all given souvenirs in a folder. One of these souvenirs was a small notepad. It was nothing special, just a plain, small pad of paper. Some got white, some

got pink. I got pink. On the
bus ride back to the school an
extremely large black girl asked
me to trade my pink paper with
another girl who had white
paper. I didn't think much
about it. It was just paper,
but I told her I wanted my pink
paper. Who would have thought
it would have turned into such a
big deal? Again, Dayton Public
Schools were way different.

     The next morning at school,
before school started, this same
extremely large black girl
decided I was going to pay for
not giving up my pink paper as
silly as that sounds. She came
up to me and started shoving me,
accusing me of being mean to her
friend by not giving her my pink
paper. She was very large, and
I was very small, and I was
certainly not violent. Luckily
the situation was instantly
noticed by our gym teacher who
broke it up right away, thank
goodness. I was scared but the
situation had been resolved.

She was taken to the office, and I went to my classroom.

Everything was fine until after school. I came out of the school building and was getting ready to get on the bus when I overheard this same extremely large, black girl telling her sister that I got her suspended. Her sister, who was a girl in my class, said, "Kick her ass!" As I'm innocently walking to the bus this girl ran up behind me, grabbed my long, blonde hair, and tried to pull me to the ground ready to "kick my ass." Luckily, again, this was broken up instantly by teachers monitoring the kids as they were getting on the bus. To this day none of this makes sense to me. I didn't want to trade my pink paper for white paper; therefore, I was a target. Minus that isolated incident, I loved school. School was my respite.

My home life was the thing that was damaging my soul. Our

home life always seemed to be eventful, but definitely not in a good way. Of course, my mother and Frank were always drunk and partying. There were always people at our house, drinking and partying with them. These were definitely not people that should be around three small girls.

One of these extra creepy friends showed inappropriate attention to me specifically. He never laid a hand on me, he only made inappropriate comments. He always, always talked about how beautiful I was, and how hot I would be when I got older. I was maybe 12 at the time. I was told by this grown man that I would probably have big boobs when I get older because "short people usually do." (Hahaha, boy was he was wrong!) He was persistent in encouraging me to become a Playboy model when I got older. He didn't make these comments to me in private as you would imagine. He made these comments in front of my mother, his girlfriend, and whoever else may be around. He didn't care, but neither did anyone else. The others would just laugh about it or agree with him. I actually think it made my mother feel proud. And in my confused 12-year-old mind, the comments didn't bother me as they should have. I kind of liked the attention. I liked that my mother was proud. Looking back, could this be the Invisible Monster rearing its ugly head?

Even without the outside drunks and drug addicts, our life stayed eventful. These said events could range from a police car pulling up at our house, putting Frank in the back, and taking him away. Or waking up in the middle of the night to Frank pulling a flaming mattress through the house and out the front door. I even woke up once to the sound of him standing in the hallway at the top of the wooden staircase peeing down the stairs. The neighbor on the other side of the duplex pulled a gun on him on our front porch once because he was running his mouth to her in his drunkenness, and I kind of remember something about him kicking her cat. Oh yeah, I almost forgot about the night I woke up to the sound of breaking glass, a lot of breaking glass. He had broken the front window to get in, and while trying to climb through he fell directly onto a glass coffee table that was sitting in front of the window.

All-in-all, regardless of the madness, I didn't think things were that bad. There were fun times too. We still spent quite a bit of time with my mother's best friend, Bonnie, and her daughter. We shared a community garden space with them in Tara. Gardening had always been a huge deal with my mother and still is to this day. My mother was mostly home at night. We didn't mind if she was drinking as long as she was at

home, she was typically a happy
drunk anyways. Then Frank left.

23 ~ Oak Street, Dayton Ohio
(Seventh Grade)

After Frank left things were different. Conveniently, there was a bar at the end of our street called Skinners, and it would become my mother's "new home" for the next year and a half. We typically wouldn't see her until the morning when we were up getting ready for school. She was usually passed out on the couch, so we only physically saw her. She never got up while we were getting ready for school. It makes sense though. When you stumble home from the bar at 3:00 in the morning it's rather difficult to be up at 6:00 with your children.

I started seventh grade at Stivers School for the Arts. Middle school was different than elementary school. In elementary school, your school was assigned. In middle school, you were able to apply to the school of your choice, and there were a lot to choose from. A few of my friends, India included, chose Stivers School for the Arts so I followed suit. In order to attend this school you had to apply, choose an art, audition, and be accepted. I chose to audition for the choir program and was accepted. Looking back, I wish I would have chosen something else. I could have chosen theatre. I could have chosen art and photography. I already had a fascination with photography and one of the art teachers constantly tried to persuade me to switch art programs. I stuck with choir. My singing voice was okay, and it greatly improved with the mandatory weekly private lessons which were part of the curriculum, but I could have flourished in one of the other art programs.

Stivers School for the Arts was by far the coolest school I have ever attended, and I absolutely loved it. The school was only seventh and eighth grade but was still quite large. We still had all the regular classes, math, science, etc., but the art programs were the focus. The arts to choose from were endless; band (multiple styles), strings, dance, theatre, choir (multiple styles, including chamber choir), all the fine arts and graphic arts, photography, and probably more that I can't think of. Every single student for every single art received weekly private lessons in their chosen art. The young talent that walked the halls of Stivers School for the Arts was off the hook!

Even though the art programs were amazing the thing I really fell in love with was the building. Having been built in 1908 it started as Stivers High School. It didn't become a middle school until the mid-80s. My grandfather actually attended high school there. The building itself was a work of art. The architecture was grand and beautiful. It was six stories high. The huge front doors opened up to a small lobby with a giant marble staircase with large brass railings leading up to the main level. This was the theme throughout the entire building. It was breathtaking.

Stivers was also said to be haunted. I knew the story; it was even featured in a published collection of Ohio ghost stories at one point. The building was six stories including the basement, but the basement was off-limits. There used to be an indoor swimming pool in the basement. In the 1920s a teacher was found dead floating in the swimming pool. The swimming pool was eventually filled in, but her ghost was said to still haunt the building. I never saw her, and if she was there haunting that building I never felt scared or threatened. Although I did fall down the stairs once and land face first, or rather nose first, onto one of the large brass handrails. I jokingly said that she pushed me down the stairs, but I was only kind of joking. I fell while coming down from the top floor computer lab on one of the end staircases, on my way to the first floor. I can't really explain what happened, but on the top step of floor two, I started to get dizzy. I stopped and steadied myself, then prepared to continue on. I thought I was okay, but I wasn't. It became shockingly apparent I wasn't okay as I fell halfway down the staircase, only stopping because I was able to grab the railing, catching myself after my face hit. Blood went everywhere, people were screaming, I was screaming. Someone found India and she came rushing to me, screaming and crying just as hysterical as I was. I was okay, I never went to the doctor to see if my nose was broken. I'm fairly certain it was though. But honestly, I was more upset about getting blood on my new shirt.

India and I had become inseparable. We spent all of our time together, she was at my house or I was at hers. Although our situations were different India's home life was also difficult. Her father was really old and was a binge drinker. I remember him selling his blood on many occasions and using the money for alcohol. That made for some really interesting, and sometimes violent, evenings. I once witnessed India trying to break his fingers by bending them back as hard as she could after one of these binges. Someone hit him in the head with a beer bottle and when he came home, he was covered in blood. I don't remember the events that led up to India trying to break his fingers, but she was very angry. Her mother was older but nowhere near as old as her father. Her mother was on disability, which she said was due to chronic diarrhea, but I really think there was more to it than that. I think she may have had some mental disabilities as well. She almost seemed childlike. It was apparent early on that India was the one that ruled the house.

When we weren't hanging out at each other's houses we spent most of our time in a nearby cemetery, Woodland Cemetery. We didn't go to the playground like normal kids, this was our playground. We were there day and night. It was situated on a big hill that overlooks the city of Dayton. The cemetery was huge and had tons of history. The Wright Brothers are buried there, at the very top of the hill, since they were Dayton natives. We picnicked on their graves quite often while looking out over the city. We would swim in the gross duck pond during the day and at night we would light candles and try to talk to spirits. We never had any real spiritual experiences, but we always managed to freak ourselves out anyway. I had friends in the past, but India was different. She was the first person that really knew me. We shared so many experiences together, good and bad, and developed an unbreakable bond.

Although I had always taken care of my sisters, after Frank left this time, things changed drastically. I felt that I had become Scarlett's primary caretaker, and Dani's primary caretaker when she wasn't with her dad. I always made sure they had food to eat. I know I didn't do everything right, but I did it to the best of my 13-year-old abilities.

I would steal Food stamps from my mother when she was gone or passed out. I would walk to Kroger's with my little sisters in tow so we would have food. I always tried to make it special for them. I would let both of them pick out their own two-liter of Big K pop, and I would allow myself one too. This did, of course, make for a long, heavy walk home. I didn't care, my sisters were happy. We brough backpacks for our hauls; I would carry two two-liters, Scarlett would carry one, and Dani would carry the bread and bologna.

I never realized the extent of how screwed up things really were until I was much older. This was my norm. I never complained. I just made sure my sisters were safe and happy to the best of my ability, and in the process, I had become quite fierce. I once came out of the house to find a couple older boys near Scarlett across the street in the alley. I'm not even sure exactly what they were doing, but they were surrounding her. I did not like it one bit. My first instinct was to pick up a brick that was laying in the grass on my way to the alley, which I did. I ran as fast as I could with that brick in my hand. I ran towards the older boys and watched them scatter like cockroaches as I got close. I didn't have a plan, I just reacted. I wasn't thinking about my safety, only Scarlett's, and I was totally prepared to beat those boys down with that brick. No one messes with my sisters!

On one occasion a Dayton Police Officer knocked on our door. Of course, my mother wasn't there, like usual. It was just my sisters and me. The police officer wanted to take Dani. He said she was really sick, and he had to take her to the hospital. He kept referring to her as a Daniel though, and it didn't feel right. I kept ensuring him Dani's name was Danielle, not Daniel. The police officer was very persistent, but so was I. I stood my ground in the doorway and did not let him in, nor did I let Dani out. I was not going to let him take her. He eventually gave up and left.

Nothing about this made any sense. Why would a police officer come to pick up a little kid to take them to the hospital, especially when one who wasn't even sick? Why would a police officer insist on taking a little kid without talking to her parents first? And why was there no social worker there to assist? You would think at the very least a social worker would be there. I'm not sure why I was so insistent that she stay with me. I just knew I couldn't let him take her. Looking back, I'm not even sure if he was a real police officer. He may have been trying to kidnap her, but I can't say for sure. Dani was safe with me and that's all that mattered.

Most of the seventh grade was a blur. I went to school and took care of my sisters, and myself. With our mother being gone most of the time I learned to take care of everything as it came up and then moved on. I escaped an attempted kidnapping once and never even mentioned it to my mother. Just another day in my life. Occasionally, I would have to run off drunk men I would find leering into our windows in the middle of the night when my mother was at the bar. I would just deal with whatever was in front of me and move on, and somehow through the madness, I remained a happy kid. I did everything in my power to make sure my sisters were happy too.

I once threw a huge surprise birthday party for Dani; I believe it was her sixth birthday. I orchestrated the entire thing because I knew my mother wouldn't do anything. I invited all my friends because I didn't know any little kids, but that didn't matter. That just meant more 13-year-olds to help make Dani feel special. Cake, presents, streamers, balloons, and a slumber party, all after jumping out and yelling,

"SURPRISE!" when her father dropped her off. My mother was at the bar, so she missed everything, but WE had a blast. Dani was so surprised and so happy. Success!

I know I said I would deal with things as they came and move on, which usually was the case with outside stressors. I also said that I would do anything to protect my sisters, but that does not mean Scarlett and I didn't have our moments. We actually both were quite fierce and maybe just a little crazy and violent at times. We were kind of like "wild animals" if you really think about it, with no supervision or guidance. And yes, I'm bossy too. After the surprise birthday party, my friends and I were cleaning up the mess. Scarlett was always easily distracted so she wasn't helping. I walked by her with a broom in my hand while trying to sweep the floor. I slightly tapped her foot with my foot as I walked by, although she would say I kicked it, and told her to start helping. That sent Scarlett into an angry outburst causing her to pick up an ashtray from the coffee table. I was on the other side of the room by this time, and I really didn't expect her to throw the ashtray at me. She did throw it, right at my face. It hit me right in the middle of my forehead then fell to the ground and shattered. Not only did it hurt, but Scarlett also made an even bigger mess. Remember that broom in my hand? With blood running down my face, and in a blind, violent rage, I beat her with that broomstick across her back over and over again while she was laying in the fetal position crying until my friends pulled me off. This was definitely not the last time that blind, violent rage took over me when it came to Scarlett.

Sisters are interesting, we can beat the crap out of each other and still be best friends

the next day. But just let
someone else lay a hand on
either one of my sisters, then
we're going to have some serious
problems. It doesn't matter who
you are, even if you're my
mother. I think we all have a
little violence in us that comes
out on occasion. Although my
mother was typically non-
violent, even her violent nature
creeped out occasionally. Other
than controlled spanking when we
were young, which I'm sure we
deserved, she very rarely laid a
hand on us. I think that's why
we were so surprised when she
was violent.

I have no idea why she was
so angry this time, but my
mother was yelling at us and
kicked the back of the rocking
chair Scarlett was sitting in.
The rocking chair had a wooden
frame with a wicker seat and
back, so when she kicked the
chair she actually kicked
Scarlett in the back through the
wicker. Scarlett started
screaming and I reacted. I

instantly pounced on my mother.
I didn't hit her; it was more of
a tackle. She was much bigger
and stronger than me, and she
was drunk, but I didn't care.
My mother got really mad then!
She overpowered me, grabbed me
by the front of my shirt
slightly choking me, and got
right up in my face and said in
a low growl, "I'm going to kick
your ass."

In her drunken state, I was
able to break free and get away
pretty easily. I ran out the
back door and hid in a bush in
the backyard. She chased me out
the door but didn't see where I
went. I watched her walk around
the house and yard, but I stayed
right where I was. She was
yelling angrily at first, but
after a while, her tone changed,
and she sounded sad and
regretful. I think she realized
the magnitude of what she had
just done. I honestly don't
think she meant to kick
Scarlett, just the chair, and
Scarlett just got hurt in the

process. I'm sure she didn't
expect her 13-year-old daughter
to attack her though. I stayed
in the bush until I no longer
saw or heard her. When I
cautiously went back inside the
house I realized the reason I no
longer heard or saw her was
because she left and went to the
bar.

The summer after seventh
grade I had my first "real"
boyfriend. He was a skater
punk/rocker which I believe is
what planted the seed for my
lifelong "rocker" mentality and
attraction to skater punks. We
spent quite a bit of time
together, he and his friends
would come to my house, or I
would go to his house. This was
all new territory for me. The
first boyfriend I had was only
my boyfriend in title, I never
even talked to him directly. I
had never even kissed a boy
before him, and when I did kiss
him it was only a quick peck.
He later called me lame and
broke up with me because I

wouldn't really kiss him. Oh well!

I would like to think I didn't know better than to have my boyfriend in the house with no supervision. Supervision was not something I was used to, and right or wrong I made the decision to let him in the house. And I was caught on more than one occasion. Once Stuart came to pick up Dani and he found my boyfriend there. Stuart had always been a scary individual and after a brief encounter with him, my boyfriend ran out the back door and hid behind the garage of the vacant house next door. Stuart left with Dani and I let him back in. I never heard anything else about that particular incident.

When my grandma caught him there it was a totally different story. My grandma was dropping groceries off for us and bent over to give Dani a hug. While bending over she had a clear view of my boyfriend hiding

under the dining room table.
She never said a word, but I
could see the disappointment in
her face, and that was
punishment enough. I never
wanted my grandma to be
disappointed in me. She
obviously told my mother at some
point. My mother didn't come to
me as a concerned mother, she
came to me full of rage. In her
fit of rage, she smacked me in
the face, called me a whore, and
told me I would be pregnant by
the time I was 14. Did she not
realize how far off that was
from the truth? My boyfriend
had already broken up with me by
that time for not French kissing
him. I actually could have
really used her love and comfort
during my first heartbreak, but
I was way beyond expecting
anything from her.

I started my period that
summer, but instead of going to
my mother and having a heart-to-
heart I just collected a bunch
of pennies, wrote a note,
stapled it a million times

because I was so embarrassed, secured the pennies and note in a little pink wallet, and took the wallet to India's house. India wasn't home so I just gave the wallet to her dad. I didn't tell him what was in the wallet or what it was for. I just asked him to give it to her when she got home. He did exactly as I asked, and India brought me pads a little bit later. India already started her period so I knew she could help. I didn't tell my mother for a very long time. India just made sure I had what I needed.

Later that summer Scarlett and I went to visit our father for a short time. Previously India had come with us when we visited our father, but this time he said no. He had recently been separated from Renee and an extra person was just too much to deal with at the time. Ultimately, Renee couldn't handle living with my brother which is what lead to their separation. It's interesting, I don't remember being in West Virginia at all. I only remember how much things had changed when we got back. India had become a completely different person. While I was gone India started hanging out with some of the ghetto neighborhood girls. She was drinking with them, smoking cigarettes and weed, and having sex. We were 13! India and I were still close, but it was clear we were moving in different directions.

24 ~ Oak Street, Dayton Ohio
(Eight Grade)

I was so happy to go back to school. I was starting eighth grade. I had friends from the previous year. I was back in choir. School was the only place I could truly be a kid. It didn't matter how bad things were at home, and things were extremely bad, I was happy at school.

My mother was sinking deeper and deeper into her drunken depression. She was so drunk and so angry all the time. I honestly can't remember a single good thing about my mother during this time. She may have had a happy moment here and there, but none that I can remember. It's interesting how our brains can block out all good memories while the bad memories remain so vivid and clear.

For instance, I have no memory of my mother's friend, I mean sex buddy, hanging out. I know he was there at least for a little while because when he stopped hanging out my mother said to me, "Well, it looks like I'm back to masturbating again." Oh yeah, my mother in her drunken depression also became the Queen of Inappropriateness. Really? What kind of mother says that to her 13-year-old daughter? Only one mother that I know of, mine!

What kind of mother accuses her 13-year-old daughter of stealing her vibrator? Mine! There's nothing like waking up in the middle of the night from a dead sleep to your mother accusing you of stealing her nasty sex toys. She must have stumbled home from the bar with a plan and could only find the empty case to her vibrator. She slammed the empty case on the table in front of me while asking me what I did with it. I told her I didn't touch it and I

had no idea where it was, which
was 100% true. That only made
her angrier. I just wanted to
go back to sleep. I was so
tired. She just slammed that
empty case down over and over
again while screaming at me for
what seemed like an eternity. I
think she eventually believed me
because she stopped accusing me
and started accusing India. She
wasn't even there. My mother's
logic, "Since India is having
sex now, she must have taken
it." Somewhere in all that
madness, I told her I started my
period. I only chose that
particular moment because I knew
it would hurt her. I knew she
would be upset that I didn't
tell her sooner, but I didn't
care. I wanted her to know that
I had been keeping it from her
for months. I wanted her to
know that I felt we didn't have
the kind of mother/daughter
relationship that allowed me to
talk to her about things like
that. She was hurt. She gave
up and finally let me go back to
sleep.

This was an interesting time in my life. Everything was changing. I was becoming a woman and figuring life out all on my own. I had a new boyfriend, but I only saw him at school. He introduced me to French kissing, and I liked it. That first kiss was so overwhelming that I literally fell off the ledge I was sitting on. I wasn't expecting the kiss, so when it happened I was surprised. I leaned in too much and fell right off the ledge, straight into his arms. We laughed, then kissed again. I was hooked and we started kissing every chance we got. I loved school, and I loved kissing!

Over Christmas break that year Scarlett moved to West Virginia with our father. I think it was her choice. Moving to West Virginia never even crossed my mind, nor was it ever discussed. Even though Dani still spent a lot of time with

her father I had no intention
whatsoever of leaving her. When
my father came to pick up
Scarlett he was expecting to
pick me up as well. He was
surprised when I told him I
wasn't going, and I was
surprised that he thought I was.
Looking back my mother probably
wanted me to go and was trying
to send me too. I can't say for
sure though. My mother was at
the bar when my father came so
she wasn't available to clear up
that minor detail, nor was she
there to see her daughter off
who was moving to a completely
different state. When my mother
returned home from the bar late
that evening I'm sure she was
surprised to find me there sound
asleep.

25 ~ Wyoming Avenue
Dayton, Ohio

My mother and I were eventually evicted from our house and we had to move in with her ex-boyfriend, the same ex-boyfriend that had left us multiple times. He had a small one-bedroom house, still in Dayton. It was actually pretty close to where we lived so I was still able to walk to school. I just had to walk a little farther, but I didn't mind. I liked school so it was worth the extra mile or so.

The setup wasn't ideal. Since it was a one-bedroom house I slept on a mattress on the floor of the only bedroom, my mother and her boyfriend's bedroom floor. My mother's boyfriend quit drinking sometime after he left so he was home and sober after work with me every day. I honestly couldn't tell you where my mother was. She may have had a job somewhere during the day and then would stop at a bar on her way home, but I really couldn't say for sure. It's odd, but memories of my mother during this time are very limited. Maybe I have just blocked out any normal memory of my mother being home at that time, or she really wasn't there. I think she really wasn't there.

I had a mandatory choir concert one evening. It was my grade, and I took my grades and responsibilities seriously. Dani was with me that day for a visit, and of course, my mother wasn't there. I had to be at school at a specific time. I had no choice but to take her with me. We walked the miles to my school so I would be there on time, me in my nice dress clothes. I had no idea how this was going to work. I needed to be on stage, and I had a seven-year-old little girl to worry about. I couldn't just leave her alone. Luckily my boyfriend, the same boyfriend that had recently introduced me to French kissing, and his friend had after-school band practice that day and they were still there. My boyfriend offered to watch Dani so I could be on stage. My boyfriend, his friend, and Dani all sat in the audience and watched me perform. It was nice. I didn't have to worry about Dani, and for the first time since I started attending Stivers School for the Arts, I actually had somebody in the audience to see me. After the concert was over my boyfriend and I snuck away while his friend watched Dani. French kissing was new to me and we did a lot of it.

I walked home with Dani, in the dark, in Dayton. I'm sure I carried her on my back a good bit of the way. It was a long walk, and it was very cold, but as we walked home, I was on cloud nine. I had a beautiful concert. I had people in the audience to watch me. I got to

kiss my boyfriend. Life was
good, until we got home, but
wasn't that usually the case?

I walked in, still on cloud
nine, with my sweet sister in
tow, and a smile on my face. I
was completely caught off guard
by the verbal attack of my
drunken mother. She was angry
that we weren't there when she
got home from wherever she was.
I was wrong for taking Dani out
at night and walking so far with
her. It was dark when we walked
home, and I'm sure it wasn't the
safest thing to do. What choice
did I have? I had to be at
school and she never came home,
so I had to take Dani with me.
I couldn't leave Dani alone and
I couldn't miss my concert.
School was important to me and
the concert was part of my
grade. I tried explaining to
her that I had no other option
but to take her with me since
she wasn't home, but none of
that mattered to her in her
drunken rage.

For no reason whatsoever I broke up with my boyfriend after that. He was always nice to me and I know he liked me, but I broke up with him anyway. This became a lifelong pattern and struggle for me, pushing people away before they get too close. It makes sense though. By this point, I had already moved 15 times in 14 years. With each move, I would make new friends, become close with these new friends, move shortly thereafter and never see them again. That's not even counting the internal turmoil caused by my absentee mother, or my siblings leaving one by one, and all the temporary men in my mother's life, my father included.

I started dating my old boyfriend, the same skater punk/rocker that called me lame and broke up with me the previous summer. He was all about me now. I guess I was no longer lame because I had kissing experience. He came to visit me often, but I never let

him inside. We would sit
outside and hang out. We didn't
go to school together because he
was in high school and I was
still in eighth grade, so the
evenings were all we had.
Hanging out outside with my
boyfriend was so much nicer than
sitting on the couch and
watching TV with my mother's
boyfriend. This was me being a
typical 14-year-old girl and
doing typical 14-year-old girl
things. I think that's why I
loved school so much. At
school, I was able to be
"normal." I broke up with him
for no reason, too.

My first experience with
alcohol, or at least my own
personal consumption of alcohol,
was during this time. Scarlett
was in town visiting so it must
have been over spring break. We
were spending the night with our
friend, also in Dayton. While
there, this friend suggested we
sneak out after her parents went
to bed. I was 14 and Scarlett
just had her 12th birthday. I'm

not sure how old our friend was
but she was somewhere in that
range. We left her house late
that night, met her friend down
the road, and walked a couple
miles to a grocery store that
sold liquor. I was not a thief,
I never have been, and I can't
even say for sure I knew what
our friends were doing, but by
the time we left they had a
variety of miniature liquor
bottles in their pockets.

There was an apartment
building across the street from
the grocery store. It was a
single building with multiple
floors, one floor being a
basement/laundry room. This
laundry room is where we decided
to spend our evening. How in
the world did we decide this was
a good idea? Four young girls
spending the night in the
basement/laundry room of an
apartment building, in Dayton,
with alcohol was actually a
horrible idea and was extremely
dangerous.

Early on we were going back
to the grocery store when we had
to use the bathroom, and they
probably stole more liquor on
those pee breaks. Rather than
continuing to walk back and
forth we eventually decided to
designate a pee washer, and of
course, we thought this was
hilarious. We peed in the
designated washing machine all
night, one of our friends even
pooped in it. I can't imagine
the poor soul who found this
nastiness when they came down to
do their laundry. We were
horrible!

Early in the morning, we
walked back to our friend's
house, parting with the other
friend along the way. We walked
in the back door thinking we
would be able to sneak in
unnoticed and go to sleep.
Wrong! We were met by our
friend's sister warning us that
their mother was pissed. She
was up all night and had no idea
where we were. Their mother
busted into the room yelling at

us, and rightfully so. She wouldn't let us go to sleep because she was up all night worrying about us and now, she had to go to work. It was only fair that we had to stay up too. She left for work, and we went to sleep.

My mother must have been informed of what we had done, and she, in turn, told my father since he was in town and Scarlett was living with him. Or possibly my father was informed, and he told my mother. Either way, they both knew what we had done, and their reactions were so completely different it is almost comical. It's no wonder they divorced so many years ago.

My father was very angry and made a huge deal about what we had done. I never knew what Scarlett's punishment was when she got back to West Virginia, but my punishment was to write an essay about what I did and why it was wrong. When finished

I was to mail it to him in West
Virginia. I didn't do this
because I thought it was stupid,
and I felt that he had no
authority over me whatsoever.
My mother, on the other hand,
came home from the bar to find
me lying on the couch, feeling
like poo. With a smile on her
face, my mother said to me,
"Your first hangover," like she
was proud of me or something.
Yep, completely different
reactions from my parents.

I didn't feel that my
father had authority over me at
that time, but unbeknownst to me
that would be changing soon. A
catastrophic, life-altering
event was right around the
corner that would ultimately
change the course of my life
forever. It wasn't a decision I
made; it was made for me. I
didn't want to go. I didn't
want to leave Dani, but someone
decided it was in my best
interest to go. My mother was
in no condition whatsoever to
care for me. Whoever this

decision-maker was probably
saved me. I see that in the big
picture now, but when I was 14
years old my already chaotic
world somehow managed to rise to
a whole new level.

I can't say that my mother
and I had a good relationship,
but this night things were
changed forever. I was home
after school, like always. I
finished my homework and waited
for my mother's boyfriend to
come home. He didn't come home,
so I made dinner and waited. I
ate my dinner alone and watched
television for a while, still
waiting for him to come home.
He never came home so I went to
bed. I had school the next day,
so I didn't want to stay up too
late. Sometime later that
evening I woke up to the sound
of my mother screaming. She
wasn't screaming at me; she was
screaming at her boyfriend who
was asleep in their bed. She
was screaming, "How many times
did you have sex with my
daughter?" She was hysterical

and continued to scream this
over and over again. I had no
idea why she was screaming this.
I was asleep and I thought I was
the only one home.

The screaming continued as
she was smacking his bare chest,
but I don't remember hearing his
voice, just hers. Through her
screaming, I became more aware
of the situation. He was
sleeping naked in their bed with
me on a mattress on the floor at
the foot of the bed. I had no
idea he was even in there. I
was asleep whenever he came
home. He had quit drinking for
a little while but that evening
he decided to go out drinking
after work and had gotten pretty
drunk. Honestly, I'm not sure
if he even knew I was in the
room in his drunkenness, but
regardless of whether he knew or
not, he was naked in the bed
with me in the room. My mother
continued to scream at him, now
saying that his penis was hard,
which was her "proof" that we
had sex.

I still don't remember ever hearing his voice. My mother decided she better ask me since he wasn't answering her. My mother's exact question was, "How many times did you have sex with Frank? How many times did you have sex with him?" It wasn't the question of a concerned mother, but more of an accusation. I was in shock. I couldn't believe she had just asked me that question. My only response was, "Mom, that's disgusting!" First of all, I was a virgin, and second, the man she was accusing me of having sex with was her boyfriend, and third, he was NASTY with a capital N-A-S-T-Y!! Remember the black fingernails? How dare she ask me a question like that?

She turned her rage back on him and started smacking him again. He was still lying down, but he had reached his limit. He jumped out of bed and started punching her in the face. I had reached my limit too. I ran. I ran out the front door. I didn't stop to get dressed. I didn't even stop to put on shoes. I just ran, in the middle of the night, in Dayton, with no shoes, or even a destination in mind. I ran to get away. I ran away with my mother's boyfriend pounding on her face.

I am so thankful for my childhood best friend, India, and I'm so thankful she only lived a few miles away. I ran to her house in the middle of the night and banged on the door until her parents answered. I didn't even have to say anything. They just let me right in. I curled up on the couch with India and undoubtedly put my ice-cold bare feet on her nice, warm legs (she always let me do that) and went right to sleep.

The next morning India and I got up and got ready for school. India typically missed

a lot of school, but she was
going that day. She was
probably only going because I
was there, and I was going to
school. We always borrowed each
other's clothes so getting
dressed wasn't an issue, but I
didn't have my backpack. Maybe
I had homework to turn in, or
something important that I had
to have for school. I was
intent on getting my backpack
before we went to school. I
really was a good girl. All I
wanted was to get my backpack so
I could go to school.

India walked back with me
to get it even though it was in
the complete opposite direction
from our school, but when we got
there no one was there. Someone
should have been there because
it was early. No one was there,
and the door was locked. We
tried the other door and all the
windows with no luck. India
even threw a rock at the glass
of the front door trying to
break it so we could get in.
The window didn't break so she

got a bigger rock, but I
wouldn't let her use it. I
didn't need my backpack that
bad. We decided not to go to
school.

   We hopped on an RTA (public
transportation bus) and headed
downtown. We transferred to
another bus downtown and rode
for quite a while. We went to
some guy's house, or trailer
rather, outside of Dayton.
Maybe it was a guy India was
dating, I don't remember for
sure. We spent the entire day
there, yet I have no memory of
being there. I only remember
being on the bus. I'm sure I
was in some form of shock from
the previous night's endeavors.
I just wanted to go home.

   By the time we got back to
Dayton, it was early evening. I
decided to walk home although I
didn't know what to expect when
I got there. I didn't know if
anyone would be there, or if I
would be able to get in, but I
didn't know what else to do.

Someone was home, but it wasn't my mother, only my mother's boyfriend. When I walked in the door he said, "Pack your bags. You're moving to your grandparents until school gets out, then you're moving with your dad." I emptied the contents of my lone dresser into a few brown paper grocery bags and waited for my grandparents outside. I received this shocking, unwanted news in an extremely cold manner from my mother's boyfriend, and my mother wasn't even there. I have no idea where she was, nor did I care. I just took my few belongings in my brown paper bag and my cat and moved to my grandparents.

26 ~ Grandparents' House #2
Kettering, Ohio

The school year was almost over, a couple months at most, so I finished my eighth-grade year at Stivers. I was supposed to catch the RTA by my grandparents' house, then transfer to another bus once I got to Dayton to finish my trip to school. Instead of transferring buses I got off the bus near my old house and walked the rest of the way to school. This was my familiar route, and I desperately needed something familiar in my chaotic life.

Everything about that time was a blur. My uncle, his wife, her son, and two cats were temporarily staying there as well. She was in the military and they had recently returned from Guam. They were nice. They would pick me up from school sometimes, so I didn't have to ride the bus.

I hadn't seen or spoken to my mother since that horrible evening when I ran away. I'm not even sure where she was. My grandparents didn't talk about her or the events that led me to live with them again. I have no idea if they even knew what happened. It's hard to say what my mother told them about that night if anything. They never asked me, and I never told them. It's possible they thought I was being unruly and just ran away. I was so used to being bounced around from place to place, from person to person, that I just accepted my situation and moved on. I never questioned it; I just went where I was told to go.

I only saw my mother once before the end of the school year. She came to visit me so we could talk. She never mentioned her accusations. She never apologized. She did however tell me that after I ran away that night her boyfriend pulled her out the front door and down the concrete stairs by her hair, breaking her ribs in the process. I told her in an extremely cold manner that I didn't care, and I really didn't. In no way, shape, or form do I support men hitting women, but these were extreme circumstances. With her, and this situation I truly did not care.

Most of my clothes were in pretty rough shape and I needed something nice to wear to my upcoming eighth-grade graduation. Part of my plan during this visit was to ask my mother for money so I could get something to wear. My father was paying court-mandated child support that was coming directly out of his paycheck. I knew she was still getting $75 a week from him even though none of her children were living with her. I felt sure she would give it to me. I pleaded my case with her, "The money is supposed to be for us, you don't even have any kids with you, I need something nice for my graduation." She said no without hesitation. I honestly don't know why I thought she would give it to me, she was notorious for taking money that didn't belong to her.

I once had to miss a super fun, end-of-the-year school field trip to Kings Island because my school fees weren't paid. Since Stivers was a school for the arts, and part of the curriculum was weekly private lessons, there was a small $50 fee to attend. My father gave me the money to pay the fee, which I gave to my mother. I should have just taken the money to school and turned it in myself, because it was never paid. I can't even count the times my father gave my mother money for school clothes that was never once used for school clothes. I should have known she wouldn't give up any of that $75 a week.

This was the last time I saw my mother before I moved to West Virginia although my actual move was still a few weeks away. At the end of our visit she asked me if I was coming back when the summer was over. It had already been decided that I was going to be staying with my father. I knew I could not stay with her any longer, nor did I want to. I told her I was staying in West Virginia. She stormed off without even saying goodbye. I didn't know at the time, but this would be the last time I would see her for the next couple of years.

Seeing how heartbroken I was my uncle's wife decided to take a special interest in me. After this visit with my mother, she took me to Value City to pick out, and pay for, my graduation outfit. She fixed my hair, did my makeup, and made sure my outfit was perfect for that evening. I was not used to that at all! I was not used to having nice, new clothes, and I definitely was not used to someone doing my hair and makeup. I felt like a princess. She made sure that I looked nice for my special day.

My graduation day was also the day I moved to West Virginia. My father had driven up to Ohio for my graduation. I had all my belongings packed up and ready to go once the graduation was over. The ceremony was very emotional for me. Not only was I leaving the school I had attended the last two years uninterrupted, but I was also leaving all my friends, including India. I was leaving Dani, I was leaving my grandparents, I was leaving the state of Ohio. I was leaving everything familiar in my life. At the close of the ceremony four extremely talented African American boys performed "End of The Road" by Boyz II Men, which was a top song during that time. I always loved that song, but this performance hit me hard.

It really did feel like this was the "end of the road."

After my graduation, we went back to my grandparents to load my stuff up into my father's car so we could start the trip to West Virginia. We waited a little while before leaving in hopes that my mother would come by to tell me bye. She had already ignored the invitation to my graduation, but I still thought she may at the very least come to see me off. She didn't. And honestly, I didn't care. The thing I was having trouble with was leaving Dani. I couldn't bear the thought of her going back and forth between her father and our mother without me there to keep her safe. After my father loaded all my belongings in his car, including my cat, he informed me it was time to go. I lost it then, I couldn't leave Dani! Standing in front of my grandparents' house in hysterics, I refused to get in the car. How could I leave her?

She needed me! But what choice did I have? I was only 14 and I had to go. After the last incident with my mother, I knew I couldn't stay with her anymore.

My Aunt Karen, whom I had always been really close with, stopped by my grandparents' house to see me before I left. She knew how things were. She knew how close Dani and I were. She could see that my heart was being ripped from my chest because I was being forced to leave Dani. She could see my pain. I don't know if she already had this plan, or if she just decided while seeing my reaction to leaving Dani, but that night my Aunt Karen promised me she would take care of her. She promised me she would keep Dani safe. I didn't know exactly how she was going to keep that promise, but I believed her. I got in my father's car and rode in silence the entire way. I accepted my fate.

27 ~ Afraid of the Monsters

My father lived in a small, two-bedroom apartment. When he first moved to this apartment it was only him and my brother. Later Scarlett joined them, and now I was there. My brother had one bedroom and my father had the second bedroom, Scarlett and I slept on the floor in the living room. We had a dog named Precious and my cat that I brought from Ohio. It was very crowded. I missed Dani so much, but this is where I lived now.

Shortly after I moved to West Virginia my brother and I were up late watching a movie in the living room. It was just the two of us, Scarlett was at a friend's house and my father was in bed. My blankets were laid out on the floor since that is where I would be sleeping anyway. I got comfortable under my blankets, ready to watch the movie. My brother sat on the

floor next to me and asked a
question that completely caught
me off guard. "Do you remember
what we used to do in the
woods?"

I had just been delivered
into the hands of the Invisible
Monster.

Part II

"The strongest oak of the forest is not the one that is protected from the storm and hidden from the sun. It's the one that stands in the open where it is compelled to struggle for its existence against the winds and rains and scorching sun."

~ Napoleon Hill

28 ~ Kolasi, West Virginia

He asked me if I remembered
what we used to do in the woods.
I knew exactly what he was
talking about, but I said I
didn't. I didn't know why he
asked me that. I definitely did
not want to talk about it. I
thought it was weird, but I
didn't put too much thought into
it. I wasn't scared or
concerned at all. We started
watching the movie, with me
lying on the living room floor,
and I guess I fell asleep. I
vaguely remember waking up and
hearing a weird noise. I didn't
know exactly what it was, and I
went right back to sleep. When
I woke up again, I realized
exactly why he asked me that
question. I woke up to him
leaning over me with one hand on
one of my boobs, and the weird
noises I heard were coming from
him. He was pleasuring himself
while sitting next to me on the
floor. I didn't say anything, I

just got up and went to his empty room to get away from him. He followed me into his room and asked me in a concerned tone, "What's wrong?" I was so confused and half asleep, so my only response was, "I want to sleep in here." Of course, I couldn't go back to sleep though. And I realized why he had asked me that question, he wanted to recreate what we had done. I didn't tell my father or anyone else for that matter. I was used to trauma and chaos, but this was different. This was the night I became afraid of my brother.

I hadn't forgotten, but I also hadn't thought about it in a long time. I hadn't lived with my brother for over four years, and during those four years, I barely saw him. I experienced so much during that time away from him, so any thoughts of him were pushed to the back of my mind. I wasn't thinking about Scarlett being with the Invisible Monster

without me there to protect her
for the last six months. My
life had just been turned upside
down. My heart was broken from
being taken away from Dani. My
mind was preoccupied with
starting over in my new life in
West Virginia.

Shortly after I got there,
I woke up one morning to find my
cat missing. When I asked my
father about it, he told me he
took him to the animal shelter
while I was sleeping. My father
was never a fan of cats. He
didn't want the cat there and
thought it would be easier if he
took him to the shelter while I
was sleeping. It may have been
easier for him, but him alone.
I was crushed! Not only had my
entire life been turned upside
down, now I had to grieve my cat
as well. I really don't think
he realized the magnitude of
what he had done. I loved that
cat, but more than that my cat
was a comfort to me. I had
taken him with me from Oak
Street to Wyoming, to my

grandparents', and then to West Virginia. I desperately needed consistency, and my cat provided that. And then he was gone.

My brother played football and my sister was a cheerleader. They both had practice all summer in preparation for the upcoming football season. Playing sports, or any other extracurricular activity, was never something I was able to do in my previous life. I always wanted to take gymnastics or attend the modeling school that India went to, but that stuff costs money. Since school hadn't started yet my father decided I needed something to fill my time. I was required to choose a sport once school started. My father decided that I would spend my free time volunteering at the same animal shelter he had just taken my cat. I hated it! I didn't see my cat; he may have already been euthanized. It was heartbreaking to be there, but not just because of my cat. I couldn't handle being around all those animals knowing that at least half of them would die and knowing there was nothing I could do about it. After a few visits, I refused to return.

Despite the rough start, it was actually quite an exciting summer. I was still sad. I missed Dani so much, and I was grieving my cat, but like always I tried to make the best of it. I had a good friend from the YMCA Day Camp that I had stayed in contact with. Her mother was my father's secretary, so it was easy to stay in contact. I was invited to go to Hilton Head, South Carolina with them for their family vacation. This was the first time I had been to the beach, or even stayed in a hotel for that matter. It was so exciting, and so much fun. My absolute favorite part of the trip was going on a dolphin tour and seeing those beautiful creatures up close and personal.

My father also decided to go to Myrtle Beach that same summer. Rather than my friends taking me all the way back to West Virginia we just met my father somewhere along the way. I loaded all my vacation supplies into his car, then headed back to the beach. These two beach vacations back-to-back were quite different though. In Hilton Head, we stayed in a nice, beachfront resort. At Myrtle Beach, we camped on the beach in a tent. I didn't mind though, other than feeling like I couldn't get clean. I love the beach, but I always feel dirty while there (even when staying in a clean hotel). So, staying in a tent at the beach I felt extra dirty, but we still had fun.

When we left Myrtle Beach. Rather than going home, we went straight to Canaan Valley State Park, located in the Appalachian Mountains in West Virginia. My father's company had a hunting/ski cabin there which all employees were able to use. It was called The Tin Benders Inn. Air Systems was a sheet metal company, so the name of the cabin I always thought was a clever play on words. The cabin was very basic, and really wasn't very nice, but we had everything we needed. Although I had just spent the last two weeks at two different beaches and had a blast, my first trip to the mountains was surreal. Never in life had I seen such a beautiful sight. It brought me back to my early days, being a forest kid, in the foothills of the Appalachian Mountains in southern Ohio. I was completely at home in the mountains.

We spent our days hiking through the mountain range in Canaan Valley, Spruce Knob, and my very favorite, Seneca Rocks. Seneca Rocks is a natural sandstone formation that rises 900 feet above Seneca Creek. Round trip the hike was only three miles, but it felt like 100 miles just to get to the top. But after you made that "100-mile" trek to the top it's totally worth it! The view from the top is absolutely stunning. You can see miles and miles of mountain tops in all directions, and everything is so green as far as you can see. I fell in love with the mountains on that hike to the top. The way down was a different story, or rather once we got to the bottom. My father locked his keys in the car! We weren't able to just hop in the air-conditioned car after our mid-summer, "100-mile" hike. Instead, we sat in the heat, exhausted, and waited patiently while my father figured out what to do next. We eventually got the car unlocked with the help of a fellow hiker that just happened to have a metal coat hanger in their car. All-in-all, it was a good vacation though, even with the key incident.

Once we got back to Kolasi, I invited my friend I had just gone to Hilton Head with to stay

the night. I don't know what I
was thinking. Actually, I know
exactly what I was thinking. I
was thinking that I wanted my
friend to come over and stay the
night. I wasn't thinking that I
was bringing her into a
dangerous situation by exposing
her to my brother. After
staying up late, hanging out,
doing girly things, we
eventually fell asleep. I was
horrified by what I woke up to.
I woke up to my friend yelling
at my brother to get away from
her. My brother was bothering
her while she was sleeping. I
never saw her again, nor did I
invite friends over to stay the
night anymore. It was horrible
enough that my sister and I were
prey to this Invisible Monster,
but every friend that spent time
at our house became prey too.

Scarlett was already
established in Kolasi and she
had a lot of friends. Those
friends became my friends by
proxy. That is when I met my
new best friend, Rhett. Just

like my previous male best friend, Rhett was gay. We spent every minute together the rest of the summer, we even had matching outfits. I ended up dating his older brother briefly, then moved onto his brother's best friend. I really didn't have much respect for the men in my life, other than my gay friends, and my boyfriends were no different. I broke both of their hearts back-to-back, for no reason like usual.

Prior to school starting, I met my next boyfriend at a pre-season high school football scrimmage. Since Scarlett was starting middle school that year my only friends were middle schoolers until this point. He was the first person I met that I would be going to school with. I actually fell for this one, but he fell even harder, so I broke up with him. This was the start of our two-year, off-and-on relationship.

I started ninth grade at
Kolasi High School. Let me tell
you, after spending the last few
years at Stivers Middle School
for the Arts in Dayton starting
school in small-town Kolasi,
West Virginia could only be
described as culture shock. The
high school was about a fourth
the size of my middle school.
Everyone seemed to be rich and
there were literally two black
people in the entire school, and
they acted white. I was once in
the crowded lunchroom when I
witnessed one of the two black
people walking by a group of
rednecks. He was nice and
polite, and while maneuvering
through the crowded lunchroom,
he lightly placed his hand on
the shoulder of one of the
rednecks and said, "Excuse me,"
while walking by. I watched
this redneck bitch shutter in
disgust and say, "Gross, nigger
germs." What kind of school had
I just started? As different as
this school was, I adjusted. I
made new friends, I broke a few
more hearts for no reason. The

worst, by far was the one that told me he loved me. My response was, "No, you don't," and then I broke up with him.

Sometime in the fall, we moved into a new house, still in Kolasi. It was bigger than the apartment but still only had two bedrooms. There was, however, a small bonus room off the living room that my father was able to use as his bedroom. We had way more room. We had a big, nice yard that we were able to put a trampoline in. Scarlett and I spent hours on end jumping on that trampoline. We jumped in the snow, the rain, we didn't care. On occasion we would even put dish soap on the trampoline when it was raining to make it extra slick; now that was fun but also responsible for a few sprained wrists!

We spent every Friday at my brother's football games. Every Sunday after church Scarlett cheered at the midget league football games. Oh yeah, my father started taking us to church, which I completely rejected. I believed in God, I just hated him. If God is so good, then why has my life been so traumatic? Why would he let us suffer like that? We went out to eat often. We spent a lot of time at the YMCA, swimming, playing racquetball, messing around in the gym, and whatever else was available to do. I started running track in the spring, which I loved even though I wasn't very good.

I had never really experienced life like this before. We were very poor, but my father did amazing things with his small income for our benefit. I believe child support checks were still being taken out of his paycheck at this time, as well, so my mother was still receiving $75 a week. But somehow my father managed to provide what we needed, even without that extra $75 a week. He tried really hard to give us a quality life. Even though we were poor, it was still way more than I was used to. Life was pretty good except for one small detail. The Invisible Monster is always lurking in the dark.

Since I ran track in the spring, I decided to run cross-country in the fall. Again, I loved it, but I sucked at that too. I didn't care. I have never been very competitive anyway. That fall, when school started, I also signed up for a class called Advanced Gym, which was basically a weight-lifting class. I was hooked! I continued to take Advanced Gym every semester throughout the rest of my high school career. I always knew I was strong, but I just didn't realize how strong until I started lifting weights. I am a very small person, very, very small. I am 5' 1" and weigh around 105 as an adult. So, as you can imagine, I was a small child too. I somewhat attribute my strength to the bias I received from the world, me being a tiny little girl.

People treated me as a fragile little girl, but I was anything but that. My max bench and squat numbers were higher than most of the girls in the class even though I was the smallest. The class was open to 10th, 11th, and 12th grade, so I was also one of the youngest, at least that first year. I really enjoyed that class. I didn't know at the time, but this was the start of a life-long passion.

I really missed Dani, but we were able to visit fairly often. Dani was living with our aunt, Karen, and her two children. My aunt kept her promise to me. While I was adjusting to my new life in West Virginia things were getting pretty chaotic back in Ohio. Child Protective Services had stepped in because Dani's elementary school had concerns. I didn't know any details at the time, I just knew Dani was living with Karen. I was told years later someone from school found Stuart and Dani sleeping in his car in the school parking lot early one morning, whether that's true or not I have no idea. I'm not sure why they would have been sleeping there. Stuart went to prison again shortly after that incident, but for something completely different. I think it was another drug charge, maybe. My mother was in no shape to care for Dani, and after a discussion with my grandparents, she agreed to let Karen have her.

Every time we visited Ohio I stayed with Karen and Dani, and Karen's two children. Her son's father was the owner of White Sail, the bar my mother worked at when I was younger. He was the guy with the Star Wars van. Her daughter had a different father, who was also in prison, for stabbing someone, I think. She was the youngest and was also the biggest brat I've ever known. Dani was the oldest of the three, but just by a year. Dani did well here.

She did well in school, she played soccer. She seemed to be happy, and seeing her safe and happy made my West Virginia life much easier.

I also visited India when I was in Ohio when possible. Her life had drastically changed as well. She became pregnant when she was 13. Despite her age, India was an amazing mother! India and her daughter were eventually removed from their home and placed in a foster home together. This was the best thing that could have ever happened to them. They were together and ended up in a really good foster home. India was once interviewed by the local news while she was still in high school about how good of a mother she was, and how well she was doing. She really was a good mother, but her daughter had a bit of a wild side. A little comical behind the scenes twist to that news story, while India was downstairs being interviewed her daughter was upstairs in her room literally catching her closet on fire! After the news people left India went upstairs to check on her daughter and found the closet blazing. She was able to extinguish the fire, and everyone was okay, but if the news crew had stayed just a little longer their news story may have been a little different.

India went on to finish school, then nursing school. She bought a house and raised her daughter in a loving quality environment. India's daughter later died in a car accident when she was 20 years old, but that's a whole other story that comes along with confusion and a rant against God. It didn't make sense. I felt that that little baby girl saved India's life. Why would God give her that baby to save her, and then take her away after only 20 years? It didn't seem fair.

During one Ohio visit I
spent the night with India and
her daughter, who was still an
infant. Scarlett and my brother
were staying with our
grandparents. I knew the
Invisible Monster was present,
but I kept it tucked discreetly
in the back of my mind. And
more than that, it was only my
experiences with the Invisible
Monster that were back there. I
wasn't worried about Scarlett.
I was just enjoying my visit.
For reasons I can't explain
though I woke up in the middle
of the night thinking of
Scarlett. I wanted to call her;
I mean really, really wanted to
call her. It was the middle of
the night, four o'clock in the
morning to be exact. I remember
thinking to myself, "That's
silly, I know she's asleep." I
didn't call her. I went back to
sleep. When my grandmother
picked me up the next morning
she told me something happened.
She didn't expand at all, but I
knew my brother did something.
Why didn't I call? I knew

something was wrong! Why did it never occur to me that my brother was abusing Scarlett too? I should have known, and I should have protected her better. Scarlett was a very heavy sleeper, which actually made her an easier target.

I was dealing with similar experiences with the Invisible Monster during that time, but at least I was a light sleeper. I would like to think that I woke up every time and put a stop to it, but there's no way to know for sure. My poor sister, Scarlett, was heavy sleeper. It makes me sick to think about him being anywhere near her while she was sleeping. She only woke up when he started to get too far, so to speak. When she did wake up, she would be in an extreme rage, kicking, screaming, hitting. She was absolutely insane if she was woken up, and that was not contained to my brother. She was like that to me too. It wasn't until I was much older that I realized why she was like that.

A little flashback story: When we were younger, maybe 11 and nine, although I'm not really sure. Scarlett and I were staying the night with our friends, actually the same friends we got drunk with in the laundry room of the apartment, but it was much earlier than that incident. Scarlett had fallen asleep, and our friends thought it would be funny to put toothpaste on her face. I did not want them to do it whatsoever, and I tried hard to talk them out of it. They did it anyway. Scarlett woke up and rubbered her eyes, smearing the toothpaste in her eyes. Her eyes were burning. She was in pain, could barely see, and she must have thought I did it. Of course, she was angry. Who wouldn't be? In her fit of rage, she rushed towards me ready to attack. I punched her in the face, knocking her flat on her back. And honestly, I

don't remember what happened
next other than the fight was
over. She continued this
nighttime rage throughout our
entire childhood and teenage
years. She was like a demon
possessed. I spent many nights
laughing at her when her demon
came out. I would venture to
say she still has it just a
little bit today, but today I
understand the cause.

I never told anyone what I
was dealing with at home. I had
friends, both guys and girls,
that I spent a lot of time with.
I just pretended like everything
was fine, but I knew in the back
of my mind it wasn't. By this
time, I knew the Invisible
Monster well. I tried to be
cautious, but occasionally it
still got me. The last time I
remember changed me. I was in
my bedroom on the phone with a
friend one evening while my
brother was playing Super
Nintendo, which was also in my
bedroom. It got later and
later, yet my brother continued

playing video games. I didn't
tell him to leave. I just
stayed on the phone. I was
trying to keep my friend on the
phone until he left, but he just
kept playing. I eventually got
off the phone and fell asleep.
I'm pretty sure my brother was
waiting for me to fall asleep
because the image that came next
haunts me to this day. What he
did to me was mild, he only had
his hands on my boobs…again.
But seeing him lingering above
me in the faint moonlight coming
through the window, wearing his
stupid WVU sweatshirt, and his
stupid ugly 90s metal frame
glasses is an image that is
burned into my permanent memory
like a photograph.

I didn't attack him as
Scarlett would have. I just got
up and went to my father's room,
asking if I could sleep in
there. He asked me what I was
doing, and I only told him
Gerald was in my room. He
instantly jumped up and went to
my room. My brother fled my

room, grabbed a wooden crucifix that my mother had made a long time ago and sat in a kitchen chair. Him, holding that crucifix made me so angry. He didn't care about what he had done. He only cared that he got caught. I don't think he was praying or asking God for forgiveness. I felt like him holding that crucifix was for show. My brother did not deserve God's forgiveness.

I begged my father to kick him out. I cried, I pleaded, I screamed, I yelled. My father refused to kick him out. He just wanted to have a discussion about what had transpired. During that discussion I asked my brother about Scarlett and Dani. I already knew he was abusing Scarlett. I needed to know if he had ever abused Dani, too. He admitted to abusing Scarlett but swore he had never touched Dani. In my experience sexual predators never admit to their crime unless they are caught red-handed. Gerald had been caught red-handed with Scarlett, but not with Dani, therefore he denied it. I was so angry. I knew he was lying but I had no proof. I told my brother that night that I would kill him if I ever found out he had done anything to Dani, and I meant it. He knew I meant it which is probably why he denied it so vehemently.

My father's solution to our problem was to attend family counseling as a group. I didn't want to be anywhere near him, and I definitely didn't want to go to group counseling with him. The second part of the solution was for Scarlett and me to lock our bedroom door at night. Seriously? I never understood why my father didn't kick him out. Scarlett and I were not safe, but my father chose my brother's feelings over our wellbeing. I knew then that my father didn't care about our safety.

29 ~ The Repercussions

I continued to do well in school. I continued to run track and cross-country. I continued on my weight-lifting journey. I continued to keep my secrets hidden from the world. I continued to live in fear. But I also was starting to show repercussions from the last 15 years. I started getting a little wild, and since Scarlett always did everything I did, she came right along with me. We did not feel safe in our home. We knew our father wouldn't protect us from the Invisible Monster. Add that on top of all the trauma from living with our alcoholic mother. Yeah, we got wild.

With our bedroom door being locked at night it made it quite easy to climb in and out of the window without our father knowing, and we did so often. One of my high school best friends, Brent, lived about a mile down the road, so we would walk there most nights. We would just sit on his couch and play Mortal Combat, watch movies, or whatever. Scarlett usually walked down there with me, but only to sleep on the couch next to me. I think she was afraid to be at home without me. I never told my friend why we wanted to be there, and he never asked. We were just hanging out.

I started drinking with Brent often, but usually just on the weekends. My brother joined the ski club and had ski trips every Friday, which my father volunteered to chaperone. Scarlett and I had friends over every single Friday they were gone, and alcohol was usually involved. Alcohol was usually involved, until the time it wasn't. We typically didn't have trouble getting alcohol because Brent had older brothers. During one of those Friday ski trips, sitting on the floor of our bedroom with Brent, and a couple other friends, he informed us he couldn't get alcohol. He immediately followed with, "But I do have this bag of weed," as he pulled a half-ounce of marijuana from his coat pocket. I wanted the alcohol, but whatever. Let's do it! And so, starts my lifelong relationship/struggle with weed.

I had my first sexual experience when I was 15, at least my first sexual experience that wasn't abuse. It was with my boyfriend at the time, I broke up with him right after. My trend, people try to get close, so I shove them away. Everyone in life is temporary anyway, right? I didn't really have a lot of boyfriends while in high school, I didn't want them. I still got a lot of attention from the boys though; I just kept them at arms-length. I also learned around this time that I could use that attention to my advantage. And as always, Scarlett followed right along-

side me. Neither one of us had
any respect for the guys in our
life, or any respect for
ourselves for that matter.

Scarlett and I were
actually very mean to some of
the guys that tried to come
around, but guys are "stupid,"
and we could do whatever we
wanted. Once a guy came over,
we forced him to put a dress on
then did his makeup. We shoved
him outside after that and
locked the door. We didn't let
him back in and he had to walk
home in makeup and a dress, on
the side of busy Kolasi Road.
He came back the next day, with
makeup remnants under his eyes,
ready to hang out again. Guys
are "stupid."

We didn't stop there, not
even close! I was friends with
this guy, who I knew had a crush
on me, but I wasn't interested
at all. Like I said, I wasn't
interested in anyone. He was
actually Brent's best friend, so
I spent a lot of time with this

guy, but Scarlett and I were mean. He walked to my house one day and knocked on the back door, but rather than answering the door we just knocked back. We didn't open the door. He went to the front door and knocked, we knocked back. He went back and forth a couple times, from door to door, us always knocking back and never opening the door. On his last trip to the back door Scarlett decided to grab a hot dog out of the refrigerator. She opened the back door, threw the cold hot dog, and hit him right in the face. We laughed, closed and locked the door, and he went home.

I could go on and on with stories like this, like the time I made a guy we called "Bird Head" ride in the trunk of my car. We were going to see a fight between some guys at school, and on the way there my car really was full. He offered to ride in the trunk. "Why sure, Bird Head, you can ride in my trunk." I lost a few passengers for the ride back and there was more than enough room for him in the car, but I still made Bird Head ride in the trunk. As I said, I was mean, and I knew I had power the power to manipulate and control (and torture) guys.

Throughout my high school years I was still drinking, but I would call it more binge drinking than regularly drinking. And I definitely got caught a few times. My father once dropped my friends and me off at the movie theatre. Once he was gone a car full of guys picked us up and took us to some junked-up trailer out Vintroux Hollow, pronounced "Venture Holler." We drank a bottle of liquor while there, then went back to the movie theatre to be picked up by my father. We thought we could hide the fact that we were drunk, and we were very, very drunk. My father was going to pick us up at the fast-food restaurant that was nearby, so we clumsily made our way there. I vaguely remember passing out sitting on the toilet in the restroom. My friend had to wake me up. My father picked us up and there was no hiding how incredibly drunk we were. I remember whispering to my friend in the back seat, or trying to whisper in my drunkenness, "Shhh, don't' let Dad know we're drunk." We dropped my friend off at her house and she stood at her front door forever. I'm surprised my father didn't walk up to the door to let her parents know what we had done. She eventually went in, so we left.

My father was very angry, but he was never one to yell. Or rather it took a lot for him to yell. He tried to talk to me, but I flipped out. I went into an extreme, hysterical fit of rage. I yelled, I screamed, I cried! All my anger and rage was bursting at the seams and that night, with all that liquor in my system, I let it out. My father stuck me in the shower, with my clothes on, to try to sober me up and calm me down. That shower only made me angrier. I hated living there! I was afraid of the Invisible Monster! My father refused to protect us! I was angry very angry! I eventually calmed down and went to sleep.

The next morning my father took me to breakfast before school. Remember the whole essay about why what I did was wrong that I was supposed to write after the apartment laundry room incident? He took a different approach this time. This time his approach was in the form of graphs and charts. My father pulled out a pen and notebook. He proceeded to draw a line graph of my life. "This is the path you are supposed to be on, and this is the path you are on." At this point, I just thought he was a dork. The next thing he did pissed me off though, but I didn't find out about it until after school at track practice.

At the beginning of track practice (my friend from the previous night ran track too), my track coach started with a lecture. The lecture was to the whole team, and he was relaying the events of the previous night, MY events of the previous night. He never used our names, but we knew exactly what he was talking about. He went on to say how shocked and disappointed he was, and that he never would have expected that behavior out of us. My father told my track coach everything. Now, that made me angry! When I confronted my father about it, he said only said, "I was talking to my friend." This was kind of true. My father was very involved with the football boosters, I think he was even the president once, so my father definitely knew everyone in that small-town school. But he wasn't just telling "his friend," he was telling my track coach, and that felt like he was crossing a line.

I won't say by any means I was proud of my behavior. I was actually quite embarrassed and ashamed. Not just for the drinking, but the fact that the drinking brought out my feelings. I had spent years stuffing down my feelings. I had spent the last 15 years in survival mode, and there's no room for feelings there. I actually thought I was broken because I couldn't cry. I literally went years and years without shedding a single tear. I had been hysterical and angry plenty of times, but the tears never flowed. Being drunk that night, all my feelings came. My tears flowed.

I didn't stop drinking. I just didn't get caught as often, and when I did get caught it's because I acted stupid. I once left school shortly after I got there with some friends. We went to some guy's house and started slamming Zima. We did this for the next few hours and then went back to school at lunchtime. I was by far the drunkest of the bunch. One of my friends, the only other female there, tried to straighten my hair and make me look presentable in the car on the way back to school. There's no way I could have hidden how drunk I was, so we probably would have gotten caught anyway, but for some reason, someone from the school office was looking for my friend that morning. When they couldn't find her they asked her brother where she was. He said she should be at school, but if they can't find her then to ask me if I knew where she was; they couldn't find me either. Of course, I knew where she was because we were together getting drunk. We were caught by the vice principal when we walked through the door. I honestly don't know if he knew we were drunk. We only got in trouble

for skipping and were sent on
our way.

The class I had directly
after lunch was history, which
was taught by my weight-lifting
coach. He was old and senile,
so I'm not really sure if he
knew I was drunk, but he asked
me to pass out papers. Not just
blank papers, take one, pass it
down kind of thing. He asked me
to return graded papers, with
names on them. I had to read
the names, find the person it
belonged to, and then walk all
over the classroom to get the
graded paper to the appropriate
person. Maybe he knew I was
drunk, and he was punishing me,
but he never said a word. I was
able to complete my assigned
task without falling on my face,
with a little help from one of
my friends. And yes, the school
called my father, but again, I
only got in trouble for
skipping.

Situations like this are
not what caused me to quit

drinking though. Drinking was
fun sometimes. Then other times
after a night of drinking I
would be so ashamed of myself
the next day that I would quit
for a while. Without going into
all the details, I became very
promiscuous but only when
drinking. After that initial
sexual experience, I was drunk
every single time I had sex. I
had no respect for myself, nor
did I feel like I was respected
by anyone else. I treated sex
like a weapon to manipulate all
the "stupid" guys. It was easy
and I felt powerful. It never
meant anything to me and those
"stupid" guys would start
following me around like little
puppies. I would just kick them
away. I very rarely had a
boyfriend, but occasionally I
let someone slip in briefly, but
I usually regretted it soon
thereafter.

     At the end of my sophomore
year my father finally decided
to kick my brother out after an
incident involving Scarlett at

the cabin in Canaan Valley, The Tin Benders Inn. I wasn't there and I don't know exactly what happened, I only know that the Invisible Monster was present. My brother was a senior that year and was already 18. My father could have called the police and had him arrested. He was an adult, and it would have been on his permanent record. I really wish he would have called, but he didn't. My brother moved in with one of his friends and continued at Kolasi High School right along-side me. I actually had classes with him and had to see him every day. We never once spoke to each other. I was happy he was gone from our home, but I didn't understand why it took my father so long to decide to make him leave. I begged and begged my father to kick him out and he refused. Now, something happened to Scarlett and he made him leave. It felt like he was choosing Scarlett's safety and well-being over mine. Whatever, he was gone and that's all that really mattered, although I would rather not be forced to sit in the same classroom with him every day at school. Once he graduated high school he went to Ohio briefly, then joined the military. He was gone and Scarlett and I were happy.

I was always able to maintain my grades. I continued to run track and cross-country and take Advanced Gym every single semester. My sophomore year our county switched to block scheduling, so I only took four, 90-minute classes a day per semester. They did this to model more of a college atmosphere, I think. It made perfect sense; you end the school year with eight classes rather than the seven. My freshman year was seven periods a day the entire year. I moved on with my life. I ran road races, 5k and 10k, between track and cross-country season. I usually had a job between seasons, as well. I tried to work during cross-country season

once, but it proved to be way
too much. I would lift weights
in the morning in Advanced Gym.
I would go to practice after
school and depending on the day
would run up to seven miles, or
do hill sprints, or whatever
else cross-country practice
would entail. I would go home
after practice, take a shower,
then go to work at Fazoli's, a
fast-food Italian chain
restaurant. And that's not even
counting the actual races, more
often than not we had to travel
a good distance to those races.
I was busy, and responsible, and
exhausted, and thriving, and was
still squeezing in the
occasional drinking binge and
regrettable sex.

30 ~ Suni – The Girl from South Africa

I was so used to always being the new girl that I made a point to try to befriend all the new kids. I knew what it felt like to be new, so I tried to help make their transition easier. I made a few really close, life-long friends that way. Exchange students were no exception, I was friends with them all. I even went to a Homecoming dance with an exchange student from Brazil.

Suni was from South Africa. She came my junior year, and we became instant best friends. She was white, which I thought was interesting because she was from Africa and I knew nothing about the world. I didn't know that South Africa specifically was known to have a slightly higher white population than the rest of the continent. Suni was white and I learned something

new. It didn't matter at all
what color her skin was, I just
thought it was interesting. I
was still occasionally disgusted
by the racism I would see at
school though, as it was so far
off from my way of thinking. I
briefly dated one of the few
black guys that attended Kolasi
High School and my sister
actually had friends that were
not allowed at our house until
we broke up. It didn't matter
that his father was a pro
football player and that he
wasn't just some thug. He was
rich and was kind of a celebrity
in the area. He was a jerk, and
we didn't last long, but it had
absolutely nothing with the
color of his skin.

Suni had had two goals
while in America. She wanted to
have sex with an American boy
and smoke American weed. I
couldn't really help her with
her first goal, sex with an
American boy. But boy did we
smoke some American weed. Up to
this point, I only smoked

occasionally but now I was hooked. It made sense though, I had basically been high since conception. My mother once told me we liked it when she smoked weed when she was pregnant with us, although I'm not exactly sure how she came to that conclusion. Add that to the lifetime of contact buzzes from living in a cloud of secondhand weed smoke, yeah, high since conception. And holy crap, Suni and I had fun!

I laughed more than I had ever laughed during that time period, but of course, it was partially weed-induced. It was so much more than that though. I felt free! The Invisible Monster was gone. A giant weight had been lifted off my shoulders when my brother left. This was the first time ever I felt like a normal "kid." I didn't have to lead a double life. I didn't have to keep secrets. So Suni and I smoked a lot of weed…and we did a lot of laughing.

We kind of floated around
from group to group, but we were
always together. Let me
introduce one of our favorite
friends, Mr. Shirde Von
Wartenberg; he was just as
"interesting" as his name. He
always managed to catch us
completely off guard with his
behavior, but not necessarily in
a bad way. He enjoyed the shock
factor, and he always made us
laugh. There was a blacklight
trend in the 90s, and of course,
I had one too. I had all the
blacklight posters, glowing
stars on the ceiling and all. I
even had handprints all over the
ceiling from a powder laundry
detergent and water paint/paste
that Scarlett and I made, which
glowed in the blacklight as
well. Another thing that glows
in the blacklight is the ink
from a highlighter. After a
short trip to the bathroom, with
a highlighter in his pocket, Mr.
Shirde Von Wartenberg dropped
his pants to expose two glowing
eyeballs drawn on his testicles

in highlighter ink. Although he always did things like this, it was never of a sexual nature. It was purely to make us laugh. And we laughed!

Suni and I did everything together. We attend junior prom together with a group of friends, Brent, Shirde, their girlfriends, and our dates. Prom was fun, but I ditched my date right after. The deal was dinner before prom with my friends, and after prom with his friends. I really didn't know this guy well and we did not have common friends. His friends were the pizza and potato chips in their parents' basement kind of friends. I politely ate some pizza, thanked my date for a lovely evening with a handshake and a smile, then bounced. I had to find Suni. We had some party hopping to do.

I say we did everything together, but there was one exception to that. Suni was a

bit of a kleptomaniac. I knew
she shoplifted a lot, but it
never involved me. We didn't
really go to the mall, or
anything like that together.
She would mainly do it while at
the mall with her host family.
I was never into shoplifting.
Other than Food stamps, and
maybe a couple dollars here and
there from my mother, I had
never stolen anything with the
exception of acne medication
from a drug store when I was in
seventh grade. I knew she did
it, and I knew she did it often.
She would even bring me gifts
she had stolen. Then she got
caught. Her host family sent
her back to South Africa early
and I never saw her again. I
was crushed, I was heartbroken,
but I was used to it. Everyone
in my life was temporary.

I lost Brent around this
time too. He was still around,
just different. Brent was doing
a lot of acid at the time. I
tried it once with him but
didn't care for it (I tried it a

few more times down the road).
I was content with just smoking
weed and the occasional drinking
binge. Brent did it a lot
though. While tripping one
night he thought one of his
friends was turning into a demon
right in front of his eyes. He
asked his friend if he was the
devil, and he confirmed that he
was, indeed, the devil. Brent
tried to kill him then and
there. In Brent's panic, he
fled the scene. The devil had
already gotten to his friend.
Brent had to go save his
girlfriend before the devil got
to her, too. On the way there
he realized he was too late.
His only choice was to kill
himself before the devil got him
too. Brent pulled off the road
into a Value City Furniture
parking lot and headed straight
towards a tent full of furniture
in the middle of the parking
lot, some type of furniture sale
that was going on. Brent
crashed into that tent and
flipped his car. It was the
middle of the night, so no one

was there, thank goodness, but the cops showed up a few minutes later. Brent woke up lying in the parking lot. The crash hadn't sobered him up one bit. When the police officers came towards him with their flashlights shining on him the flashlights were all he could see. Brent was on his knees with flashlights closing in on him. He asked the "figures" behind the flashlights if they were there to sacrifice him. After they confirmed that, yes, that's why they were there, Brent attacked. In his tripping and violent state, the police officers had no choice but to contain him, which resulted in him receiving quite a beating. Brent was never the same after that. He became super, duper Christian and only came around to evangelize. Needless to say, our friendship fizzled out after that.

I still had friends, but I was losing the people I felt closest to, again. I was still getting a lot of attention from guys, but I hadn't changed any. Besides the occasional regrettable, drinking binge one-night stand, I preferred to be left alone. My friends were constantly trying to set me up with people, one being an exchange student from Holland that only referred to me as "Goddess." Another guy that liked me was only a freshman. I was a junior at the time and had no idea who he was. About halfway through the school year common friends brought him onto my radar. They asked me if I knew who he was, then proceeded to tell me he was going around telling everyone he thought I was the hottest girl in the school. I didn't know him, so I had my friends show me who he was. Me being a junior and him being a freshman, my response was, "He'll be cute when he gets older."

31 ~ Senior Year - 1996/97

My senior year was the first time I had been in the same school as Scarlett since that ghetto Dayton elementary school. Scarlett was in ninth grade. Scarlett and I always did things together, but we also had our own friends. This year, we became best friends. We did everything together. I got my first car that year so we could do whatever we wanted. I got my license when I was 16, but up until this point, I was only able to use my father's car when he wasn't using it. I loved the freedom of having my own car. I could go wherever I wanted, whenever I wanted...until it rained. My car was a Smurf blue 1985 Chevy Celebrity we named Shit Tank, and Shit Tank refused to start in the rain.

I really appreciated having that car, which my father bought for me. And honestly, I didn't

even mind Shit Tank's quirks.
Scarlett and I just contained
our freedom to sunny days. When
my father bought the car, we
both went to pick it up. The
car was way out at the end of a
"holler" (hollow) at a trailer.
The guy selling it was old and
dirty, but whatever. We were
just there to pick up a car. I
think I had some kind of problem
with the car right away because
my father sent me up there alone
to have that old, dirty man fix
something. While up there, the
old, dirty man started telling
me about another much nicer car
that he had. He told me he was
willing to trade cars with me
for no extra money. That makes
no sense, why would he just give
me a nicer car? I asked him
that very question. His
response was, "I'll scratch your
back if you scratch mine."
Enough said.

I didn't react, I didn't
say a word. I just let him
think I wasn't offended. I made
a plan to meet that old, dirty,

and now perverted man the next day to "exchange" cars. I loaded my car up with the biggest guys I knew, one being a giant at 6'5" and probably around 300 pounds, whom we referred to as Nate-Dawg. My bodyguards and I went to the designated place at the designated time. I knew I wasn't going to exchange cars. I don't know who that old, dirty, perverted man thought he was messing with. I was nowhere close to being that stupid or naïve. I was only there so my large male friends could beat his ass. He never came. It's possible he attempted to come but drove off after he saw Shit Tank full of big, tough guys that appeared to be out for blood.

I told my father what happened, not about the plan for the beatdown, only about what the old, dirty, perverted man said. My father called his house to confront him but only spoke to his wife. She told my father, "He promised he wouldn't do that anymore." He turned out to be a registered sex offender whose prey were young, teenage girls. Sometimes my father didn't have the best judgment. Sex offender or not, a 17-year-old girl had no business going out into that "holler" alone.

Scarlett and I spent a lot of time with Rhett, our gay friend. Rhett was younger than me, but he was always a presence in my West Virginia life. Rhett was the one boy that was allowed to spend the night with us. He wasn't openly gay, but we all knew. He just wasn't ready to talk about it yet. That doesn't mean we didn't defend him tooth and nail when someone dared to call him gay.

I had already been smoking weed quite a bit, but now Scarlett, Rhett, and I were smoking together, and smoking a lot. We fluttered around from social group to social group, always together and always high.

I had little flings here and there, but they were always short-lived, and I was always the one who ended it. I wasn't drinking alcohol that often because I really wasn't happy with my promiscuous behavior that came along with it. I was completely content sticking to smoking weed and hanging out with my friends.

Being in West Virginia there were plenty of back roads and parking spots we frequented. One of our favorite, known spots was called The Penis Tree. The Penis Tree was located just off one of the narrow, back roads which traveled over a small mountain in Kolasi. Just as you start to ascend the hill, immediately to the right, is the Penis Tree. Its name is no accident. This tree was quite large, as was the "penis." Protruding from the tree was some type of abnormal growth which was an exact replica of a penis, minus the testicles. We parked there often, smoked weed,

and laughed at The Penis Tree.
But then again, we were always
laughing. If we didn't have
anything to laugh at, we would
create something to laugh at.
"On the count of three let's all
start laughing," works
surprisingly well.

Early on in my senior year,
I reconnected with one of my ex-
boyfriends. He was the
boyfriend that I broke up with
because he told me he loved me.
We dated for four months when I
was a freshman and he was a
junior, which was the only long-
term relationship I ever had.
It had been a couple years, but
there was obviously still a
connection. He picked me up
after climbing out my bedroom
window one night and we drove to
a secluded area. We had sex,
which we had not done while we
were dating during our younger
days. It obviously wasn't my
first time having sex, but it
was my first time having sex
where there were feelings
involved and it scared the crap

out of me. The next night I
climbed out the window again
with the intention of spending
the evening with him. I walked
across the street and got in the
cab of his truck. He instantly
leaned over to kiss me. I
panicked. I don't even know
why. I can't explain it. I
stopped him, jumped out of the
car, and went home.

He came over the next day
to talk to me about the night
before. We sat outside while he
told me his theory. He said he
thought I was afraid to get
close to people. He was exactly
right! It had never occurred to
me before. I never understood
my behavior. I had spent the
last 17 years in survival mode.
I obviously had severe
abandonment issues. I was a
victim of sexual abuse. I
didn't trust anyone. I felt
like every single person in my
life would hurt me, because most
of them had. I shoved people
away once they started getting
too close. It was a defense

mechanism; I just didn't realize it at the time. I shoved them away before they could hurt me. I didn't know why I did the things I did. I didn't understand that my behavior was the result of my lifetime of trauma. His theory was a profound concept in my mind, kind of like an "ah-ha" moment. I finally understood. He helped me that day, but even with my newfound understanding, I was still done spending time with him. Just because he was able to figure out my problem and put it into words doesn't mean my behavior changed.

32 ~ The Bad Influence

I became friends with a
girl that was a year older than
me. She was in college and she
liked to drink and drink a lot.
It really upsets me when I think
about how often I rode in the
car with her after a night of
drinking at the bar. Even
though I had plenty of drinking
experience I was never okay with
drinking and driving. I never
did it, but for some reason, I
was okay riding in the car with
her (she later died in a car
crash). We went to bars even
though we were under-age. Her
boyfriend was 21 so we never had
any problem getting drinks, not
that we were ever carded
anyways. I had always been
social, but I preferred to be in
smaller groups as opposed to
crowds. I typically didn't go
to a lot of parties, but with
her I did. She was very social
and in college, so she always
knew of parties going on.

My previous drinking trend consisted of me getting drunk, having an emotional meltdown or regrettable sex, and then taking a long break from drinking. It might be fun every once in a while, but then something happens, and I'm done. I was drinking way more than I was used to with my college friend, but after going to one last party with her I wanted nothing to do with alcohol.

This last party I went to with her was huge, easily 100 or more people. It was a college party, but it was being thrown by a former Kolasi student and was at his parents' house in Kolasi, so I knew almost everyone there. Of course, being in the small town of Kolasi half the people there were still in high school. I went to this party with my friend, but we were off doing our own thing. Scarlett and Rhett were there, and I had tons of other friends there, too.

One of these friends took a special interest in me. This wasn't new. I had been friends with this guy since ninth grade and he had shown interest in me in the past, we had even gone on a date once. This night though I decided I hated him, and I hated myself for being at the party, and I hated myself for being drunk. He forced me to perform oral sex on him. He held my head down and wouldn't let me get away no matter how much I tried to pull away. The only time I was able to pull away I only had enough time to vomit from gagging, then he instantly forced me down again. I physically tried to get away, but he was stronger. I'm so angry at myself for not fighting harder. I never said the word, stop. But then again, how could I say anything while being forced to do what I was doing? I should have bit his damn penis off! This was only the second time in my life I had performed that act, once on my brother (at least only once that I remember)

and now on my "friend." It was
finally over. I never spoke to
him again. I never went to a
party again. I stopped hanging
out with my college friend. My
social circle got smaller.

Although my social circle
was small, that doesn't mean it
was uneventful. I typically
stayed away from alcohol, but
one night I decided to drink
with friends. That night I was
the one that crossed the line.
I had a good friend who is by
far one of the nicest guys I
have ever known. I knew he was
attracted to me, but I was not
interested in anything more than
friendship. But that night of
drinking things went a little
further. I knew it didn't mean
anything to me, but I was
willing to do it anyway - binge
drinking and inappropriate sex.
During this time, he told me he
was a virgin. He was older than
me, and I was 18, so this kind
of surprised me. Knowing it
didn't mean anything to me
whatsoever I tried to put a stop

to it. He was such a nice guy, and I didn't want to hurt him, but he begged, and begged, and begged, so I gave in.

I wish that was the worst thing I did to him, but it got way worse. He became one of those "little puppies" that followed me around everywhere. We did spend a lot of time together, but I never let anything happen between us again. The one time he tried to kiss me while dropping me off he hit my dog with his car, which stopped the kiss dead in its tracks. My dog always got excited when cars pulled into the driveway. I had already opened to door to get out and I guess he left the car in neutral. My dog was coming to investigate, and the car started to roll backward; the open door hit her. I yelled at him for hitting my dog and went inside. My dog was fine, but he never tried to kiss me again.

It gets worse. I was never
interested in him, but he was in
college and he always had money
and weed, and he was really
nice. He felt safe, and he was
easy to manipulate. We were
always running around meeting
interesting people. He was a
rocker/skater punk, so I was
right in my element. I didn't
actually lead him on, per se,
but I never told him I wasn't
interested either. We were
never alone together, I made
sure of that. My sister and
Rhett never left my side, while
we bounced from social circle to
social circle. One bounce
landed us right into the circle
of a guy that caught my eye, and
then what I did was terrible.
This guy that caught my eye, I
started bringing him along with
me right along-side this super
nice guy who I knew wanted a
relationship with me. I didn't
even have enough respect to tell
him I was attracted to this new
guy. I took his virginity,
broke his heart, and moved on

right in front of him. That is
how I crossed the line.

33 ~ Like a Virgin

"I made it through the wilderness. Somehow, I made it through. I didn't know how lost I was until I found you."

~ Madonna

This guy that caught my eye had actually been on my radar for quite some time. This guy was the same guy that had previously stated that I was the hottest girl in the school, to which I responded, "He'll be cute when he gets older." He got older! I never forgot about him; I just went on with my life. He never forgot about me either. I was the girl of his dreams, he thought I was unobtainable, and here we were in the same social circle. There was an obvious attraction, but I was cautious. I know he thought I was playing hard to get, but honestly, I was just scared. We were watching a movie in my bedroom once, along with a group of people. I was lying in my bed and he asked me if he could join me, although indirectly. I knew exactly what he was asking, he wanted to lay down with me, but I grabbed an extra blanket and pillow and handed it to him so he could lay on the floor next to my bed. This went on for weeks. We were never alone, and other than riding on his lap in an overcrowded car once there was never any physical contact. Like I said, I was scared.

On January 7th, 1997, we decided to skip school together. We ended up at my house, alone for the first time. I don't know who made the first move, but it didn't matter. For me, our attraction had been building up for weeks, and a whole lot longer for him. Our first kiss turned into our first everything, literally everything. We are still doing

life together 24 years later,
married with two children. He
is still the love of my life and
I am still the girl of his
dreams.

34 ~ This Guy That Caught My Eye

This guy that caught my
eye, the love of my life,
deserves a proper introduction.
He was a sophomore in high
school; I was a senior. He was
a punk who got kicked out of
school regularly for fighting
and skipping school; I made good
grades and took school
seriously. He had no rules or
consequences; Although I didn't
always follow them, I definitely
had rules and consequences. He
was once dropped off at my house
by his mother on their way home
from the police station after he
was picked up for joyriding in a
stolen vehicle; I was home after
school doing homework. He was
angry and aggressive (towards
life, not towards me); I was
happy and chilled. None of that
mattered, like they say,
opposites attract. I saw
through all his rough, unguided
exterior and knew he had
greatness in his heart.

My first visit to his house was one to remember, like a scene from a movie. His house has been referred to as The Animal Kingdom, and it was just that. Upon entering the front door, the first thing I saw was half of a Golden Retriever puppy. I only saw half of the puppy because the other half of the puppy was squirming its way underneath the carpet through an extremely large, puppy chewed hole. That Golden Retriever puppy was just one of many. There was a pack of full-grown large dogs that swarmed around me as I walked through the front door. Everywhere I looked I saw cat eyes leering at me. They were on top of the kitchen cabinets and curled up in a fruit bowl on the kitchen counter. They were sitting on an old Husson's pizza box on the dining room table, literally everywhere I looked I saw a cat. There was some sort of loud screeching coming from one of the bedrooms, which I later

found out were two very loud and
very annoying Amazon Parrots.
In order to get the pack of
large dogs away from me my
boyfriend grabbed the cat out of
the fruit bowl and threw it
right in the middle of the dogs.
Their interest instantly shifted
to the scrambling cat and we
were able to break through to
the kitchen. Once in the
kitchen, with my back to the
counter, and the pack of dogs'
interest elsewhere, I was able
to take in the full picture. It
truly was an Animal Kingdom.
His mother had a thing for
taking in strays, both animals
and people. My boyfriend
already had one of his best
friends living with him. This
friend was spinning one of the
cats, a Siamese cat named Sammy,
like a propeller on the kitchen
floor. There was another Golden
Retriever puppy standing on the
couch, or squatting rather,
while peeing on the couch. I
had direct eye contact with that
puppy while it was squatting on
the couch, peeing. My look was

utter shock, the puppy's look
was, "What?!?! I pee where I
want!!" in a sassy attitude.
What a sight! I didn't know it
at the time, but I would soon
become one of those strays…but I
never peed on the couch.

35 ~ Tis' Life

My brother had been gone
for a little over a year. Life
was nowhere near perfect, but it
wasn't too bad either. Scarlett
and I had a brief glimpse of
normalcy, but like everything
else in life, it was short-
lived. We were already pretty
severely damaged; my sister was
worse than me. Or maybe we were
equally damaged we just
responded differently. I
internalized everything, and
Scarlett was very explosive.
One of these said explosions
caused me to lose my home.

The course of my life
changed forever that day. I
truly believe everything
happened exactly as it was meant
to happen, but that day I felt
like the floor dropped right out
from under me, again. It was
beyond my control.
Conversations were had and
decisions were made, and to this

day I don't know the truth of how I ended up living with my 16-year-old boyfriend after only a few weeks of dating.

One day after school Scarlett and I were at home alone. I was on the phone with my boyfriend. He was going out with his friends, so I was planning on staying home and doing homework. Scarlett was waiting for our father to get home so she could go out with friends. I don't know what set Scarlett off that day, but she was extra explosive. I just tried to ignore her and continue my phone conversation. This was pre-cell phone days, so I was on a cordless telephone, which I took outside to get away from my crazy sister. While I was outside, she locked all the doors and then unplugged the base of the cordless telephone, so my call was disconnected. Since I couldn't get in through the doors I crawled in through a window. Once I got inside she was waiting for me with a

butcher knife. I had no idea
what she was really capable of,
and I wouldn't put it past her
to stab me. I didn't try to
fight her, I just ran out the
back door with her chasing after
me with the knife, then she
locked the door behind me again.

Our father came home from
work right about that time,
finding me locked outside.
After I told him what happened
he decided Scarlett was not
allowed to go out with her
friends now. I was not okay
with that. She had just chased
me around the house with a
butcher knife. I had no
intentions of going anywhere. I
had homework and my boyfriend
was out with his friends.
Scarlett was supposed to go
somewhere, she needed to go
somewhere. I could not be
around her, but she wasn't
allowed. So, I told my father I
was going to go somewhere. I
told him I couldn't be around
her. I told him she threatened
to stab me with a butcher knife.

I told him that if she didn't leave, I had to leave. I don't know why my father was so adamant about me staying, maybe he wanted Scarlett and me to talk and hug it out. Maybe he wanted to draw a diagram of our lives and give a speech. Whatever was going on in his head he didn't share it. He had no intention of listening to reason or even trying to understand my need to get away from her. He just said, "If you leave, don't come back." I left.

When I left that day I didn't realize I was leaving for good, I just had to get away. I was barely 18 and in the middle of my senior year. My car was broken down, parked in my father's driveway, so I just walked away. I had no idea where I was going. I eventually walked to a friend's house and asked to use the phone. I called my boyfriend. He didn't have a car either, so his friend came to pick me up. We were dropped off at his house and we went inside. His mother met us at the front door and told me my father called, but she never told me what he said. She just told me I was going to live with them now. My father's last words were, "If you leave, don't come back," so I had no reason whatsoever to believe I was allowed to come back. I took his mother's words as my new reality; I was going to live there now.

I didn't make the decision to move in with my boyfriend after three weeks of dating, the decision was made for me. I was used to decisions being made for me though. I lived with my father for three and a half years in West Virginia, two of which he allowed The Invisible Monster to reside with us. I begged and begged my father to make my brother leave and he refused. I was told, "If you leave, don't come back." My brother was sexually abusing my sister and me, yet he was protected and allowed to continue. I just had to take a break from my crazy, knife-wielding sister and I was told not to come back. This never made sense to me. I believe now this could have been The Invisible Monster at work. Maybe my father protected my brother because he's just like him, only milder. Maybe my father was anxious for me to leave so he would be alone with Scarlett. Who really knows? But like I said, The Invisible Monster is always lingering in the dark. It may be dormant at times, but it's never really gone...

36 ~ He's Wild

My boyfriend was barely 16,
and he was wild. He brought me
into his wildness, and it was
exciting! Yes, I smoked weed
and was nowhere near an innocent
little angel, but he liked to
push the boundaries for sure.
He was never into drugs or
anything like that. He didn't
even smoke weed. His "high"
came from raising Hell! I never
even had a speeding ticket, yet
with him, I was running from
cops on four-wheelers. I could
tell he was well experienced in
running from cops, too. It was
actually quite impressive.
While riding on the back of a
Banshee (racing four-wheeler),
holding on tight, with a cop car
on our tail, he started
fishtailing the Banshee on the
gravel road we were flying down.
That fishtailing created a huge
dust cloud, which allowed us to
pull off the road and down into
a small riverine undetected,

under the cover of the thick
dust cloud. He turned off the
Banshee and we watched quietly
as the cop car passed through
the dust cloud and continued on.

I could also talk about the
time he drove my car right into
the grocery store. My boyfriend
dropped Scarlett and I off at
Kroger's to get a couple
midnight snacks, he was waiting
in the car. With snacks in
hand, we started walking towards
the exit as the automatic doors
opened. They didn't open
because we were walking out. We
were nowhere near close enough
for the sensors to detect us.
They opened because a car was
driving through them, my car to
be exact, a Geo Metro!! My
boyfriend was sitting in the
driver seat with a big smile on
his face, and then he blared the
horn. Scarlett and I just
looked at each other in
confusion. We didn't know what
else to do, so we just got in
the car. We backed out through

the doors of the store and drove away. He's WILD!!

   We were shot at on two occasions, although we were only truly in danger once. We liked to explore abandoned houses and occasionally we chose the wrong one. Once we were out in the middle of the woods, but the landowner must have lived nearby, because he fired several shots in the air from a pistol and said, "I called the law!" We ran through the woods, through a creek, back to the car, and drove off in a panic. The other time, we actually were in danger as a shotgun was fired straight in our direction, by a guy who was rumored to be a child molester. He frequented the local grocery store, and I'll admit, he was very odd. He would park his truck near the entrance to the grocery store and just watch people come and go for hours. He never went into the store, nor did he ever get out of his truck. There were rumors he caught masturbating to young girls from his vehicle, but who really knows. He lived in a nearby house, and my boyfriend decided it was a good idea to throw rocks at his house one evening. The child molester reciprocated with gunfire. I wanted to run, but my boyfriend laid on top of me keeping me flat on the ground until he felt like we could safely get away.

I can't say that I wasn't having fun, we found some really cool abandon locations. One of our favorites was Lakin Industrial School for Colored Boys in Point Pleasant, West Virginia, abandoned in 1956. This building had such a dark, evil history. We thought we may encounter something supernatural there, but we never did.

Another favorite was more local, The Red House. I believe it's a museum now, but it was abandoned in the 90s. It looked as though the residents had just vanished. It was a huge two-story mansion built in the early 1800s and had quite a history. There were supposed to be underground tunnels leading to the nearby river that were utilized as a part of the Underground Railroad, but we never found them. We did however find a stairwell in the basement that led nowhere. The mansion looked as though it had been vacant since the 70s, and the last occupants left everything behind. The closets were full, there were dishes in the kitchen, photographs and personal items were everywhere. There was a dentist's office and a beauty salon in the basement. We found all kinds of cool treasures there, but we didn't take much. It didn't feel right, this place really did feel haunted. Even the few items we did take felt haunted, so we took them back. There was said to be a ghost named "Sam" that watched over the place, and we felt he may have traveled with the items we took.

Most of our adventures were innocent and caused no harm to anyone. Trespassing was our biggest crime, and I was okay with that. But my boyfriend liked to push the boundaries, and I was not okay with that. My boyfriend and his friend decided to bust out a window of the house of a teacher they knew, and apparently had a problem with. It was not a preconceived plan, just a spur-of-the-moment decision they made with me in the car. My boyfriend was driving. His friend jumped out with a baseball bat and busted out the front picture window on the house of the unsuspecting, probably sleeping teacher. I had no idea who this teacher was, nor did I understand why they were doing it, but I was there. Of course, they were caught. My boyfriend was 16, his friend was 17, and I was 18. I was the adult involved and I was the one who was going to pay for their behavior. I was so upset and scared. I didn't want

anything to do with my boyfriend
if he was going to continue to
do things like that. That was
not the kind of life I wanted,
and I told him so. I believe
his parents paid off the teacher
and replaced the window. She
didn't press charges.
Everything was smoothed over and
my boyfriend never pushed his
boundaries quite like that ever
again.

37 ~ Goodbye Kolasi High School

Through all this madness I
was still going to school. I
was one elective credit away
from graduating, the second
semester of my senior year. It
was difficult. I didn't have a
car. I lost my home and was
forced to move in with my
boyfriend who rarely went to
school. I decide to write a
letter to the Board of Education
pleading my case, trying to get
permission to graduate early.
My request was denied. I wasn't
aware at the time, but my father
was conspiring against me with
my high school vice principal.
I'm not sure what my father told
him, but it couldn't have been
the truth. I was pulled out of
my science class one morning for
a meeting with the vice
principal. During this meeting
he gave me two options, "Move
back home with your father or
turn in your books at the end of
the day." I was shocked! I was

crushed! I didn't understand!
I was still at school, making
good grades, and doing
everything I was supposed to do.
Did he not understand my father
told me not to come back, that
it was not an option? I wasn't
just some unruly teenager who
refused to follow the rules. I
didn't choose to move in with my
boyfriend, I was merely told
that's what I was going to do.
Given my choices, move back home
or turn in my books at the end
of the day, I made the only
possible choice in my mind. I
turned in my books. I didn't
waste my time going to class the
rest of the day. I just
collected my things and left. I
was crushed. I was heartbroken.
I wasn't the only one who was
crushed. My science teacher had
always shown special interest in
me, and she knew I didn't
deserve that. She cried right
there in the middle of science
class as I collected my
belongings and walked out the
door. School had been my
respite my entire life. It was

the only stable thing I ever had.

I never understood why my father did that. I had been on the honor roll throughout my entire school career. I just had to get through the next two months and obtain that one elective credit and I would have been done. My father never once tried to encourage me to move back home, and he definitely never told me I was allowed. As crushing and heartbreaking as it was losing my home, and now my high school diploma, my real confusion came from my father. I felt as though he sabotaged my life. Why would he do that? I was only with him for three and a half years, two of which were filled with sexual abuse that he allowed. My father seemingly kicked me out for no reason, yet he refused to make my brother leave knowing what he was doing to Scarlett and me. It didn't make any sense. Why was it so easy to do that to me and so hard to do that to him? Why was my father so quick to inform my high school principal of my new living situation? I'm going to guess that he didn't rush into the high school and tell them that my brother was a sexual predator when he finally made him leave his senior year. If he did inform them I don't believe I would have been forced to sit through the remainder of the school year in the classes I shared with my brother. My brother should have been in jail, not sitting next to me in Spanish class. Not that I was ever close with my father anyway, but his behavior during those short three and a half years made me realize that I didn't trust him whatsoever. I was okay not being close. I didn't want to be.

I was so used to my world being flipped upside down, and I had become very resilient. I just readjusted my plan. I was used to doing that, too. There was no way I was going to go back to high school the next school year for one elective credit. I took the test to obtain my GED. I flew through the test and scored extremely well, so well that I was awarded a small monetary award to put towards my college education. That award didn't make me feel proud though. It actually made me feel like crap. Of course, I did extremely well on the test. I had already basically been through high school. That award just confirmed what I already knew, I was way better than a GED. I started college the very next semester, exactly when I would have started had I been able to finish high school. I worked a full-time job delivering pizzas for a local, privately owned pizza chain, and I managed to maintain Dean's List status throughout my college career. I was optimistic about life again without missing a beat. Fuck the Monsters!

38 ~ Somewhere Along the Way

Somewhere along the way, I reconciled with my mother. I don't remember exactly when, but I do remember exactly why. Scarlett and I were visiting our mother and her new boyfriend over Christmas break. We hadn't been around her for a little while, but I guess she decided we were mature enough to ask if we were smoking weed yet. I may have been 17 and I was definitely smoking weed. I confirmed that I was. I smoked weed for the first time with my mother, which superficially healed our relationship. She was actually fun and interesting to hang out with. She is an artist/hippie, who is highly intelligent and has had so many interesting life experiences. My mother and I actually became friends. I convinced myself I didn't need her as a mother. Being her friend was enough, at least that's what I told myself.

I would take whatever I could get!

I will not say that her environment was any different than when I lived with her, but an occasional visit was okay. Her new boyfriend was a severe alcoholic, so they were always drunk. He lived an extremely wild life before he met my mother, filled with smoking crack and violence. He didn't have any teeth because he was hit in the face with a baseball bat. He told us once, "I got new teeth, but the dog ate them." Huh? It was very interesting watching him eat corn on the cob with his gums only. I don't think he showered often. His feet were stained black, and he had long scraggly, greasy hair. He was also very abusive to my mother. I never knew if I was going to find her with a black eye from her face being slammed continuously against the wall, or to her arm in a cast from being pushed down the stairs. He was a piece of shit and I absolutely hated him, but I tolerated him because she did. He later died from liver failure caused by the alcohol.

My aunt kept her promise. My baby sister, Dani, was living with her and my two cousins. Dani's father was in prison and our mother was a mess, especially now with her new abusive boyfriend. Dani did well at first, but by the time she was 13 she was more than my aunt could handle. Dani was starting to exhibit symptoms of her trauma-filled youth. By 13 she was already having sex, drinking, and smoking weed. My aunt dropped Dani off to live with my mother and her abusive, disgusting boyfriend. I said I tolerated him because my mother did, but that's only because deep down I didn't really have that much compassion for my mother. But Dani was my baby! There was no way I could tolerate her living with either one of them.

39 ~ Another Stray - 1999

Two years into my relationship with the love of my life, still living with his mother (and all the animals), going to college, and working full-time, I brought my baby sister to live with me. I was not okay whatsoever with Dani living with my mother and her new, abusive boyfriend. In the short time she was with them the boyfriend threw a parmesan cheese can at her and called her a whiny little bitch because she was upset about whatever abuse he was administering on our mother at the time. Hell no, that's my baby! I was 20 years old; she was 13. I was so happy to have her! But what did I know about raising a 13-year-old, one who was so severely damaged? It didn't matter, it was my job to save her. I loved her more than anyone or anything in my life!

I know I did so many things
wrong, and not saving her is my
biggest regret in life. Dani
was wild, but of course, she
was. Look at where she came
from. Her entire existence was
full of trauma on top of trauma.
In her short 13 years she had
experienced the sexual abuse of
our brother. She felt abandoned
and unloved by both of her
parents. The only stability she
knew was living with our aunt
for a few years, but our aunt
was actually a little crazy and
I'm sure that caused some
unpleasantness. (She later died
of a drug overdose, which I fear
was intentional) I do understand
why my aunt couldn't keep her,
but I'm sure it made Dani feel
abandoned again when she dropped
her off to live with our mother.
I understood her damage more
than anyone, my damage runs
quite deep as well.

40 ~ Meanwhile in Kolasi

The Invisible Monster is always lingering in the dark. It may be dormant at times, but it's never really gone...

Scarlett was still in high school and alone with our father. She was experiencing her own traumas. She dated a string of non-quality guys who were no good for her. One got her strung out on cocaine and turned her into a kleptomaniac. She ended up on probation for shoplifting. And let me tell you, there's nothing quite like your high energy, flighty sister strung out on cocaine. We were still best friends and spent a lot of time together, but I wasn't involved in that part of her life. I just saw the repercussions. And then The Invisible Monster reared its ugly head.

Scarlett came home late one night thinking our father was sleeping. She went into the laundry room, which was right next to her bedroom, and took off her clothes to stick in the washer. The laundry room and her bedroom were at the opposite side of the house as our father's bedroom, where he should have been sound asleep. She stripped down completely naked, started the washing machine, then went to her bedroom. She put on pajamas which consisted only of an oversized t-shirt. After getting dressed she went into the kitchen and immediately saw our father through the kitchen window, watching her from outside. He jumped out of sight once she spotted him. She had just been completely naked in the laundry room, which also had a window. Was he watching her? What was he doing out there? It was really late. He should have been asleep. Scarlett obviously freaked out. She went outside to question him, and he acted dumbfounded. He finally stumbled out the excuse, "I was looking for the dog." Just then, the dog walked sleepily out of our father's bedroom from the other end of the house to see what all the commotion was about.

To this day our father refuses to say what he was doing out there that night. The only excuse he has ever given is, "I was lonely." I don't even know what that means, "I was lonely." Does that mean he was intentionally watching her get naked through the window for sexual gratification? Does that mean he was outside the window pleasuring himself to his daughter's naked body? Has he done this before? Has he watched me through the window too? What kind of sick man does this? I guess the same kind of man who refuses to make a sexual predator leave for the safety of his young daughters. Is my father The Invisible Monster?

Did this whole thing start with him? Was he the one responsible for our encounters in the woods so many years ago? I saw a show once where two young foster kids, a boy and girl, were forced by their foster parents to perform sexual acts on stage in front of a paying, adult audience. Were my brother and I forced to do these acts in the woods for an adult audience? Having so many unanswered questions has made my imagination go wild. Could his refusal to acknowledge what our brother was doing be due to the fact that he was getting some kind of sick pleasure from it? Why will he not talk about it?

My sister left. She bounced around from place to place for a little while, then had no choice but to go back. She graduated high school and moved away for college and never looked back. It was the best decision she ever made; she has a beautiful life.

41 ~ Dani

In the beginning, I tried to set rules and boundaries. These rules were more from a 20-year-old's perspective than a responsible adult's perspective though. No smoking weed until homework is finished. No drinking on school nights. She was going to do these things anyway, but this way I could help guide her and try to keep it under control. Forbidding it would not have worked. I encouraged her to focus on school, which is what I was modeling for her being in college. That first semester she lived with me my grades skyrocketed. I wanted her to see what was possible if she just kept her focus in a responsible direction. She was highly intelligent and always did well in school, straight A's without trying kind of person. She was so beautiful, loving, and generous. If she could have

just made it through to
adulthood, I believe she would
have had a beautiful life.

The first time Dani tried
to commit suicide she was only
14. She wasn't successful until
age 19, one month before her
20th birthday. That first
attempt was because I grounded
her for refusing to go to
school. She wasn't sick, she
just didn't want to go. Her
best friend never went to
school, nor was required to ever
go. That made it much harder
for me to get Dani to go. She
was in 8th grade. One morning
before school Dani and I were
arguing because she refused to
go to school. I eventually
grounded her. I still had
classes that morning whether she
went to school or not. After
the blowup I started to get
ready for school. While getting
ready I heard Dani in the
bathroom violently throwing up.
I ran to her bedroom and
discovered an extra-large,
empty, economy size bottle of

Tylenol with the lid off. I ran back to the bathroom to ask her if she took all the Tylenol. She did, indeed, take the entire bottle. I don't know how many pills she took in all, but it was a lot. Some people think because it was Tylenol it wasn't serious, but that's not the case at all. It may not be as quick-acting as pain pills or nerve pills, etc. Tylenol works in slow motion. It takes a few days for the toxins to fully envelop the body causing the internal organs to start failing. It will cause death just the same.

After rushing her to the local hospital she was transported to a much larger children's hospital by ambulance. She was admitted and was required to drink charcoal multiple times a day for about four days to absorb all the toxins from her body. I never left the hospital. I slept in a chair right next to her bed, or right in the bed with her. My life had always been chaotic, but the level of stress I experienced from this was on a whole new level. I loved her so much and it really hurt that she did this because I grounded her.

Fast forward to 2005, after an abortion, multiple suicide attempts, a severe Xanax addiction, living alone, and working as a stripper, Dani was successful in her suicide attempt by sitting in front of an oncoming train. 2005 was the year that broke me.

I want to start with the good; Dani had a beautiful heart and a loving soul. She was stunningly beautiful, with long reddish/brown hair and eyes the color of a shiny new penny. She was taller than me at 5'5", with a lean build, and the Boob Gods were very generous to her. She was absolutely gorgeous. She was highly intelligent and ambitious. She graduated high school at 17. She started college early and was doing

well. She was working as a
manager at the same local pizza
chain where I worked. She
usually had a side job at a car
wash, or whatever else she could
squeeze in. She was still wild,
but she hid most of it from me.
She seemed to be doing well. By
this time my boyfriend and I
were married and had one baby
boy born in 2002. The four of us
lived together happily in our
own little house.

And now the bad; Dani had
acquired the nickname, "Xani-
Dani," as in Xanax. She had
been abusing Xanax for a long
time, but it was relatively mild
abuse if there is such a thing.
While at college she met a guy.
He was bad news from the get-go.
He had a whole lot of money from
a settlement. He had a
prescription to "Xani-bars,"
which are meant to be broken at
the perforations and taken in
small pieces. With this guy,
his money, and prescriptions,
her abuse kicked into high gear.
She decided to move out after I

found a Xanax on the floor of her bedroom. My son was a toddler at the time, so of course, I was angry, but I never asked her to leave. I just asked her to do better. That Xanax on the floor could have killed my son if he found it. She didn't want to do better, I guess, so she moved into an apartment with her boyfriend.

After a brief time living with her boyfriend, he cheated on her, so she kicked him out. I offered for her to move back home, but she had a lease and she wanted to try to keep her apartment. After a couple semesters she dropped out of college and started working at a strip club as a dancer to pay rent. She continued to work at the pizza place, but only part-time. She was extremely addicted to Xanax and was drinking heavily on top of all the pills. I guess that's what it takes to get up on stage and dance naked, to be drunk and high out of your mind. And she was definitely out of her mind.

I could go on and on about Dani totaling her car in the parking lot of the strip club in the middle of the night. I could talk about her disappearing and being unreachable for days at a time. I could talk about the countless calls in the middle of the night from concerned friends when she started acting erratic and self-destructive. I have had to smooth things over with police officers who called me after finding her wandering around in the middle of the night, drunk and high. I have found her lying in a waist-high frozen field of grass in the middle of the winter wearing only a tank top and jeans. There were a couple more suicide attempts. I could seriously go on and on. Needless to say, I was under a lot of stress, and extremely scared for her safety and well-being.

I will have to say the
event that scared me the most
was actually the results of Dani
trying to do something positive.
She called me in the middle of
the day telling me all kinds of
crazy things. She told me that
her car wasn't in her driveway
and she thought it had been
stolen, among other things. She
also said someone was in her
apartment going through her
dresser drawers. She said it
was someone she knew from the
strip club. Dani kept yelling,
"Star, get out! Get out, Star!"
I could hear how upset she was.
I could hear the fear in her
voice, yet I never heard anyone
else. I told Dani I would call
her right back. I instantly
hung up and called the police.
I told them what was going on.
I told them that someone was in
her apartment by the name of
Star and wouldn't leave. A
police officer rushed over to
her apartment expecting the
scene that I had described. I
was so confused when the police
officer called a little while

later to let me know no one was at her apartment. He didn't see evidence that anyone had been there either, plus her car was in the driveway.

When I called Dani back I started to realize something was extremely wrong. The things she was describing were so far out there, so violently brutal and scary. She was describing them as though they just happened. She said one of her friends put a torture apparatus on her head, an apparatus that was used in the horror movie, "Saw." It was kind of like a reverse beartrap that is secured to the head, one-piece connecting to the lower jaw, and one-piece secured to the upper jaw. When the reverse beartrap torturing device is activated it will rip the head in half, completely separating the lower jaw from the rest of the head. And her friend put one of those on her head! After talking with the police officer, and now this, I was scared to death. Something was definitely wrong.

My husband was at work with our only car, and I was home alone with our two-year-old son. I had no way to get to Dani's apartment. Out of desperation, I called my father to see if he could go over and check on her. His office was really close to her apartment and I needed to know she was okay. He said he was too busy and wouldn't do that favor for me. I was going to have to wait until my husband got home from work to check on her. I received a call from a paramedic a short time later saying they were taking Dani to the hospital. At first, he thought she was on meth, but he now felt she was having a psychotic break. He asked me if she was schizophrenic. She definitely had problems with mental illness, but never in my life did I feel she had schizophrenia. I was so confused and so scared. I called my father back and begged

him to take me to the hospital
to be with her, which he did.

Once I got to the hospital
I was able to go straight back.
I was desperate to find out what
was going on. Nothing made
sense. While talking to her she
seemed fine. Maybe fine is not
the right word, but she seemed
sober. She told me that she was
gang-raped the previous night.
She said she was in a dirty
room, lying naked on a mattress
on the floor. One by one, guys
would come in and rape her, then
leave so the next guy could have
a turn. She said she was raped
over and over again. Did
someone slip a pill in her drink
at the strip club? Was she
roofied? The police were called
once again, and a rape kit was
done. They did all the
necessary tests, collected
samples, and took her clothes.
I had no reason to believe what
she was telling me wasn't real,
and I was pissed.

While talking with Dani, sitting in that hospital room, I watched as her pupils instantly shrank down to pinpricks. They were normal previously, but once her pupils changed she pointed to the open door and started screaming, "That's him! That's him!" I jumped up and ran to the doorway of the hospital room ready to pounce on whoever just walked by. There was no one, just an empty hallway. I ran to the nurses' station to find out who just walked by. I told them whoever it was may be the rapist. Again, there was no one. That didn't make any sense! Dani just saw someone walk by! What in the world was going on? She had to be drugged, I was sure of it. Then her bloodwork came back, along with a tox screen, clean. Not just regular clean like she wasn't roofied clean, her blood was completely clean. She didn't even have Xanax in her system. How was that possible? She should have at least had Xanax in her system since that was her drug of choice, but she didn't.

It took me a little bit to figure out what really happened that day. She didn't have a psychotic break. She wasn't schizophrenic. I learned later that Dani decided to stop taking Xanax. She knew she had a problem and was trying to do something positive. Unfortunately, she didn't go about it the right way. When you have a 10+ milligram a day habit it is very dangerous to quit cold turkey. Xanax tends to cause extreme drowsiness, so the absence of it makes it near impossible to sleep. I'm not sure exactly when Dani stopped taking Xanax, but it was long enough to be completely out of her system. I know now that she had been awake for multiple days in a row, which was causing her to hallucinate. I know now that when her pupils were pinpricks, she was hallucinating, and when they were normal, she was lucid.

I still don't know if she was raped.

To this day, this is one of the scariest things I have ever experienced in my life, so when I found out she went straight back to abusing Xanax I was crushed. She was over the withdraw and hallucinations. Why would she go back to it? I knew then that she was going to die. I didn't know how. Maybe a drug overdose? Maybe a car crash? With the prescription pill epidemic, people were dropping like flies, and Dani already totaled her car once. I lived in constant fear because I knew it was going to happen. If I was in the shower and I heard my phone ring I would panic, "Oh my goodness, Dani's dead!" I would rush to answer my phone, dripping wet, leaving a trail of soapy footprints down the hallway. I couldn't wait until the end of my shower to make sure she was okay. If my phone rang in the middle of the night my heart would start racing as I

ran to my phone in a panic. I
knew she was going to die. I
knew I would get a call any day,
it was just a matter of time.

42 ~ It's the End of the World as We Know It

On Labor Day 2005, we attended a small family gathering with Dani. She spent the entire day texting a guy she met at the strip club. She told me she thought he had given her herpes and she was going to the doctor the next day. I knew how she was, so I wasn't surprised, but I was still upset. It really concerned me that she was hooking up with guys from the strip club. It was obvious to me that was a bad idea. I knew what time her appointment was, so I met her outside of the doctor's office after her appointment to see if she was okay. I saw her coming out, so I met her at the door. I hugged her and told her I loved her. I then asked her to go somewhere with me to talk, but she said she had to go to work. I begged her not to go to work, but she refused to call off. In the parking lot, outside of the doctor's office, I said to her, "First off, you shouldn't date people from the bar." She replied, "You always tell me what to do. Do I ever listen?" Although this conversation seems mild, this was actually a harsh conversation between Dani and me. We rarely argued, and we almost always spoke to each other with respect. After saying a brief hello to my husband and son, Dani got in her car and drove away. I had no idea that would be the last time I would see her alive.

She was very angry with me, but as scared and concerned as I was, I still decided to give her a few days to cool off. Dani's doctor's appointment was on a Tuesday. I ran into one of her friends a few days later. As I was telling her about Dani's most recent friend that overdosed I started to cry. I told her I wasn't crying for that friend; I was crying because I was afraid Dani was

going to die. Actually, I was
more than afraid. I knew she
was going to die.

Friday, September 9, 2005,
Labor Day was the previous
Monday, I woke up with my two-
year son just like any other
day. We had breakfast then got
ready for a playdate in St.
Albans. On our way to the
playdate my cell phone rang. It
was an unfamiliar phone number,
so I answered quickly. I was
greeted by a police officer from
Hurricane, West Virginia. The
officer asked me if I was in
Hurricane. I told him I was
not, then asked, "Do I need to
be?" Dani lived in Hurricane
and I knew it involved her. I
was so angry as I turned my car
around and headed back towards
Hurricane. I thought she had
been arrested and I was going to
have to go bail her out of jail.
She was ruining our playdate! I
called my friend to let her know
we weren't coming, that I had to
go to the police station. She
asked if she could come to pick

my son up before I went. I
think she already suspected why
they called me, but she never
really said for sure. She just
picked up my son and I drove to
the police station.

I walked into the police
station and was instantly taken
back to a room. Two police
officers walked into the room,
one carrying a white envelope in
his hand. I asked them if they
arrested Dani, to which they
replied, "no." My next question
was automatic, "Is she dead?"
After what seemed like forever
one of the officers said, "We
don't know." I experienced a
brief moment of relief when he
said that. I thought she was
just injured, and they didn't
know if she was going to make it
yet. I was wrong, she just
hadn't been identified yet. The
police officer started to pull
photos out of the white envelope
he was holding, and I quickly
grabbed for them. He pulled the
photos out of my reach and
flipped through them before

handing me a single photo. The photo only contained the image of a dragon tattoo, one I knew very well. Dani had a very large, very distinctive dragon tattoo on her lower back, the exact dragon in the photograph I was holding in my hand. Dani was dead.

At approximately 5:39 that morning a young, unidentified female was struck by a train and killed instantly on the train tracks that run right along Main Street in Hurricane, West Virginia. Her mangled body landed next to a gazebo near the train tracks right outside the Hurricane Fire Department. She was referred to as "Jane Doe" until I identified her around 10:30 a.m. According to the train conductor, she was sitting on the train tracks with her legs facing out away from the tracks, towards the fire station. He thought she was a deer at first, but quickly realized she was a person. He said she was rocking back and forth but didn't move out of the way. I knew she did it on purpose. Her rocking back and forth like that translates in my mind as anticipation and fear. I believe she knew the train was coming and knew exactly what she was doing, and she did it on purpose.

I left the police station and drove straight home. I rushed inside, sat on the living room floor, and started screaming hysterically. Dani was dead. I knew it was coming. I wasn't surprised. And oddly, I had a small sense of relief, which came along with a whole new level of guilt. I wasn't relieved at all that she was dead by any means, but it was comparable to someone dying at the end of a long and painful terminal illness. Not only was her suffering finally over, but I no longer had to live in constant fear waiting for her to die. I did not expect her to do it so brutally though. It takes courage to sit down in front of an oncoming train, and the damage to her small body was catastrophic.

Everything that happened next was a blur, and it was pure chaos. My phone was ringing off the hook, yet I could barely form sentences. There were so many people at my house, all of our local friends and family. Eventually, out-of-staters started straggling in. Arrangements were made, but not by me. My father and her father took care of everything, which was good. I was in shock. My brain was so jumbled. When asked for my advice or opinion regarding details I couldn't even respond. I couldn't comprehend their words, like they were speaking in a foreign language. I would just stare at them in confusion. I did, however, manage to select her dress for the viewing. That task in itself was quite stressful.

Although her body was severely damaged, the visible damage was contained to the back of her head, back, and lower extremities. We were able to have an open casket at the viewing. Her internal damage, however, was catastrophic. The impact of the train instantly severed her brainstem, breaking her neck, and flattening the back of her skull. Her leg was broken completely in half, but still connected, and was up by her head. The funeral home worked their magic to make her semi-presentable, although you could still see the makeup covered abrasions on her face. In my jumbled brain, I didn't take into consideration the huge incision on her chest from the autopsy when selecting her dress. Going to her apartment was traumatic enough, and after digging through her closet to find the perfect outfit only to be told by the funeral director that it wouldn't work because it was too low cut, I was beyond stressed. After some stress vomiting, which I had done often over the years, and another trip to her apartment I was able to find a sweater to go over her low-cut dress. It wasn't ideal but I couldn't handle dealing with it anymore.

There were so many people at Dani's viewing; people I knew, people I didn't know, people I hadn't seen in many years. Bonnie, Dani's God Mother, along with her daughter were there. Family traveled from Ohio to attend; my mother included. During the viewing, in my heightened emotional state I walked up to my mother, and Dani's mother, and threw my arms around her. I even called her "mommy." In a coldness I can't describe my mother briefly placed her arms around me in a cold and distant embrace, then walked on without a word. Dani was to be cremated, so her funeral was five days later. Our mother did not attend. She didn't want to wait in West Virginia for the funeral, nor did she want to go home only to travel back five days later. Her excuse was that she felt she already said her goodbyes at the viewing.

The graveside funeral was even more massive. I have no idea how many people were there, but it felt like it was in the hundreds. I was late getting there because my son was freaking out at home. I wasn't planning on taking him to Dani's funeral because he was only two, but I couldn't leave him at home screaming and crying like that. He wasn't used to being away from me, and even though he was only two years old he knew something was drastically wrong. He was not leaving my side without a fight, and it was not a fight I was willing to have. When my husband, my son, and I finally got to the cemetery all eyes were on us as we walked up to her grave. They weren't looking at us because we were late, they were looking at me. Not a single person could or would deny that I was the one who suffered the greatest loss, and the looks were that of sympathy.

Her ashes were contained in a small, marble urn. The entire funeral mob lined up and passed the urn, one by one, down a line until the urn landed in my hands. I can't describe what it felt like holding Dani's ashes in this tiny, little marble box. It didn't make sense. It was so small. This was Dani. I passed the urn on to the next person in line, but the moment it left my hands I experienced a surge of extreme panic. I couldn't catch my breath and started to hyperventilate in front of the entire funeral mob with all eyes on me. Bent over at a 90-degree angle, clutching my chest with one hand, the other still reaching in the direction of Dani's urn being passed along, the ground started swaying underneath my feet. My vision was starting to go black as I was blindly guided to a graveside chair that was intended for me anyway. I barely remember all the people who were surrounding me, I only remember my son crying and reaching his little arms out to me. He was scared to death! My scared little baby boy who needed me snapped me out of my panic, and I sat like a statue through the rest of the funeral clutching him tightly in my arms.

It took a while to fit all the pieces of the puzzle together, but I do have a semi-understanding of the events that ultimately led to Dani sitting on the train tracks. I know from speaking with her friends that she had been calling around the previous night on the search for Xanax, her drug of choice, but could only find OxyContin. She always preferred nerve pills over pain pills, but she took the Oxy anyway. I found an empty bottle of Jack Daniels in her apartment and believe she downed the whole bottle after

her shift at the strip club.
She left her apartment with only
her phone and walked to a nearby
apartment complex where the guy
she met at the strip club lived,
the one she believed to have
given her herpes. I don't think
she left with the intention of
committing suicide. I feel like
she would have left a note as
she had in the past. I think
she was just lonely and wanted
someone to hang out with, but
she was also pretty intoxicated.
I don't know exactly what
transpired between them, but I
know he wasn't interested in
hanging out with her in the
middle of the night in the state
she was in. He refused to let
her in. His apartment complex
was located right next to the
train tracks that ran through
the small town of Hurricane,
just on the other side of Main
Street. Dani left his apartment
and sat down on the train tracks
and waited.

It really was the end of
the world as I knew it. Dani

was gone. How could that be?
Aside from my son, she was the
most important person in my life
for almost 20 years. And now I
had to live my life without her.
I was so full of heartache, and
I was even angrier! I was angry
at her parents for not giving
her the life she deserved. I
was angry at myself for not
doing more. I know I could have
done better, but her parents
should have done better first.
I was angry at The Invisible
Monster for the deeply rooted
trauma he imposed on her at such
a young age. I was angry at the
world for moving on without her.
How can people just go on with
their lives? Do they not
realize Dani is dead?

43 ~ Find a Penny, Pick it Up

"Find a penny, pick it up,
then all day you'll have good
luck." I had been saying this
since I was young, and always
picked up every penny I found.
After a conversation with my
grandmother, I started looking
at pennies differently though.
She told me every time I find a
penny to pick it up because it's
Dani wishing me good luck. I
don't know if she realized how
impactful that conversation
would be to me, then, and for
the rest of my life. I took her
words to heart. To this day,
every single penny I find makes
me smile. I pick it up no
matter where it is. I always
smile and say, "Thank you,
Dani." I get excited every time
I find one, even 15 years later.
I have vases and boxes full of
Dani pennies that I have found
over the years. I even have a
1985 penny tattoo, which was her
birth year. Interestingly, in

the 15 years since she has been gone, I have only found one 1985 penny. I check the date of every single penny I find.

I am actually a firm believer in ink therapy, too. Sure, it's not for everyone, but every single one of my tattoos are important to me and have provided me so much emotional relief over the years. Although I already had tattoos, the first one I got for Dani was shortly after her death. While collecting her belongings from her apartment I found a playing card, the joker card. It was from a deck of cards with a dragon theme, so rather than an actual joker the image was of a solid black dragon. Dani carried that joker playing card around with her until she was able to get that the dragon tattooed on her lower back. That dragon tattoo was the same tattoo they showed me in the photograph at the police station to identify her. Holding that playing card in my hand, looking

at her inspiration for her
beautiful tattoo, I decided to
get the same dragon tattoo.

44 ~ Pet Cemetery

I had been driving by the Pet Cemetery regularly since moving to West Virginia, along the main route between Kolasi and Clayton Valley. The cemetery is located on a small hill with the words, Pet Cemetery, spelled out in large stones in the grass on the hillside. I had always seen it, knowing it was a pet cemetery, so I was completely shocked when it was decided that Dani would be buried there. Since I could barely form full sentences during the decision-making process, I had no part in choosing this location. I did however question and complain when I was informed. "I thought this was a pet cemetery. Why are her ashes being buried there?" I was told that animals were on one side, people were on the other. I was still in shock, and I had no fight in me, so I accepted it. I should have fought.

Dani's ashes being placed in that pet cemetery ultimately led to a ten-year stretch of trauma, literally blood, sweat, and tears. I don't even know where to begin. Ownership of the cemetery changed hands somewhere early on, and with that change in ownership, the cemetery went downhill. The grass was knee-high, and after a slightly traumatic experience for my son who was maybe four at that time, I started to get angry. After walking through the tall grass to visit Dani's grave my son stepped on a bees' nest that was hidden by the tall grass. He ran off in a panic, being chased by bees, and ran into a small metal sign, also partially hidden by the tall grass. He ended up with multiple bee stings and an abrasion on his neck from the sign. My husband and I spent many hours there mowing the grass and weed eating around her headstone after that, and the other headstones nearby. I even coordinated work parties to do the whole cemetery. I knew I wasn't the only one that was bothered by the condition of the cemetery. The thing that ultimately pushed me over the edge though was discovering that a dog had been recently buried not even five feet from Dani's grave. That disgusted me to my core, it was so disrespectful. It felt like they put her on the same level of importance as a dog and I was not okay with that.

I started looking into having her ashes moved to a new location. This whole experience was way more than I anticipated. First things first, I spoke with the new owner about the process of having her ashes resumed. He sent me to the courthouse to file some sort of petition to have it done, which I did. He then informed me he would need to use a backhoe to dig up her remains since he didn't know

exactly where they were in the
ground. I knew exactly where
the urn was. The only place the
ground was disturbed after her
funeral was around the
headstone, logically that's the
only place it could be. I also
knew it could easily be dug up
with only a shovel, which I
volunteered to do myself. He
wouldn't take my word as to the
location, nor would he let me do
it myself. He would do it for
$200 though. I had already paid
$100 to file the petition, so
the cost was starting to add up.
I offered to donate the plot
back to him to cover the cost,
but he informed me the plot had
been purchased for only $75 and
wouldn't cover the cost. That
$75 was like a punch to the gut.
I still don't know who made the
decision to place her there but
knowing that whoever it was only
paid $75 was sickening to me.
This was just another reason I
had to get her out of there. I
will add that the owner of the
cemetery had an ankle bracelet
secured on his ankle, the kind

worn by those on house arrest and gave off a creepy vibe. I think he really just wanted my money. I did not want Dani's ashes there any longer. My husband offered to go in the middle of the night and do it, but I wouldn't let him. I could see that going extremely bad, you know, grave robbing and all.

Next-step, find a new cemetery. I decided to have her remains moved to Ohio, the same cemetery in Dayton we used to play in when we were younger, swimming in the gross duck pond and picnicking on the Wright Brothers' grave. This was also going to cost money and quite a bit more than the small fees that were already adding up. I had been speaking with my grandmother through this process and she knew how upset I was. She offered to pay for the new plot, so I continued on, trying to figure out all of the details. But shortly after my grandmother's offer a conversation with my grandfather brought my planning to a halt. He wanted to discuss paying for Dani's new cemetery plot. He agreed to pay for it, but he informed me it was only a loan rather than a contribution. My grandfather spoke of it as a business deal, very cold and with no emotion. I was crushed. I was a young wife and mother, and very poor. There was no way I could take on a debt like that. I knew my grandparents had plenty of money, so that wasn't an issue at all. He just didn't feel like it was his responsibility to pay for it. Okay, change of plans.

New plan, I was going to move forward with having Dani's remains exhumed, but I was just going to keep the urn containing her ashes for the time being. I was also in contact with Ashely, Dani's half-sister, and my ex-stepsister, throughout the process. Knowing my new plan Ashely requested some of Dani's ashes. Dani was her sister, too, so I agreed. I started looking into buying a new keepsake urn that came with four smaller urns so I could divide and distribute her remains. This new plan also came to an abrupt halt after an out-of-the-blue telephone call from Dani's father. He was appalled by the idea of me separating her ashes and divvying them up. He felt it was morbid and disrespectful, taking little bits and pieces of her and handing them out. He was right! I don't know why I hadn't thought of it like that, but now that I did there was no way I could do that. Ashely was not happy about my decision whatsoever, but I didn't care. Whether he had the authority to or not, Dani's father had given me Power of Attorney over her remains, and I was firm in my decision. I may have been a little too firm, and definitely too morbid, in my response to Ashely's continued plea for a portion of her remains. Regretfully, my response was, "What would you like? Her head? Her right arm? Maybe a leg?

What part of Dani's body would
you like?" Yeah, that may have
been a bit much. She doesn't
talk to me anymore.

I didn't know what else to
do at that point but leave her
remains there for now. I still
decided to make the best of the
situation and came up with
another new plan. I decided to
make her graveside area nicer.
We were already cutting the
grass in that area, but I wanted
to do something more. I went to
Home Depot and loaded up in the
garden section. I bought a
beautiful wrought iron trellis,
I bought flowers, annuals, and
perennials, some of which would
climb up the trellis. I bought
multiple bags of potting soil.
I even bought decorative rocks
to use as trim for the
beautiful, graveside flowerbed I
planned on creating. I went
shopping alone, then drove to
the cemetery. The road for the
cemetery was a bit of a distance
from Dani's grave and there was
no way to park any closer. With

my car loaded up, I parked on
that road and made multiple
trips back and forth, carrying
heavy bags of soil, carrying
rocks, my shovel, a large six-
foot-tall wrought iron trellis,
and tray after tray of flowers.
I carried multiple jugs of water
with the intention of watering
my masterpiece once finished.
After unloading all my supplies,
I left to pick up my husband and
son; my husband was planning to
help me with my masterpiece.

That same creepy man with
the ankle bracelet met us at our
car once we returned. He
informed us that we couldn't
place the wrought iron trellis
there, or plant the flowers, or
place the rocks, or basically
anything I had planned to do.
Once again, I was crushed, and
my husband was pissed. Could
that creepy man not have come to
tell me this as I was making
multiple trips backing and forth
across the cemetery, with my
arms full of heavy supplies?
Why did he wait until I

returned? He had to know I was
there and what I was doing. He
lived in a junked-up trailer
that was on the cemetery
property right next to the
office, both of with are
completely visible from where I
parked my car and Dani's grave.
There was nothing else to do but
load all supplies back into the
car and leave, so that's what we
did.

I was done! I had been
manically trying to figure out
how to make this work for
months, and around every corner,
there seemed to be ten new
hurdles to climb over with
boobytraps set all along the
way. I was done! I couldn't
deal with this anymore, so I
didn't. I left Dani's ashes
right where they were, in the
tall grass, in the pet cemetery,
next to the dog.

45 ~ Out of the Box

The condition of the cemetery was always on my mind and was a major source of stress, but there was nothing I could do about it. I just went on with my life. What choice did I have? I did however acquire a PTSD diagnosis along the way. They say everything happens for a reason, and sometimes I believe that to be true. Call it synchronicity. Call it timing. Call it meant to be. Call it whatever you want. Ten years after Dani's suicide I was finally able to have a small amount of peace after removing her remains from the horrible pet cemetery.

My father just returned from his second six-week trip to India in which he stayed in an Ayurvedic ashram, healing, meditating, and studying yoga. In a visit after this second trip, my father in his Zen

342

mentality commented on the location of his house. His house, although really nice with all the updates he had done, was situated on a very busy road just two miles down the road from the massive John Amos Power Plant. Every day, all day long, dump trucks full of coal passed his house on their way to the coal-burning power plant. I just happened to know someone that was currently in the market for a house, and I thought his house would be perfect. He wasn't necessarily thinking about selling his house, but he agreed to let her see it. The timing couldn't have been better. He had recently heard of a massive piece of property that belonged to a friend and was currently being repossessed by the bank. This massive piece of property was in Hurricane, West Virginia, off a string of back roads, and consisted of 78 acres of mostly undeveloped forest with a small house near the front of the property. Just like it was meant to be, my friend bought my father's house, and my father bought the 78-acre forest.

The house was livable but in desperate need of a little TLC, but the property was worth it. This was West Virginia property, so the house was nestled in a hollow near the front of the property, with a nice pond on one side of the driveway, and a creek other on the other. The small creek flowed alongside the house and back yard, then trailed off into the forest. There was a big garden near the pond and a large flat, yard in the back. Behind the house, beyond the back yard was the remaining 76 acres of undeveloped forest, a creek, and hallow running through two tree-covered hills.

I found a few walking trails leading out in the forest decided to go explore. What I found was magical! Deep in the forest, I came upon a small area where the sun was struggling to break through the tall trees. The small area was sort of like a small peninsula with the creek surrounding three sides. I can't really describe what happened to me as I stumbled upon this magical spot, but something happened as I was standing in the filtered sunlight that was struggling to get through. This place was special. I could feel it throughout my entire tingling body. My racing heart was overwhelming. I can't explain it, but I knew this place was magical. I told anyone who would listen, "I found this magical place in this magical forest," even though I didn't completely understand yet.

Around this time the pet cemetery changed ownership again and the condition of the cemetery had improved. The grass was no longer being neglected and the overall appearance was better. I think it was even operating under a different name. I was grateful.

That cemetery had caused me so much stress over the years. As I was driving by one day I saw someone cutting the grass on a riding lawnmower. I was so happy that someone was taking care of the cemetery again, and without even thinking I pulled into the cemetery. I walked up to the young man on the riding lawnmower with only the intention of thanking him, which I did after introducing myself and explaining why I was there. I told him of the stress I had endured and why I was so grateful he was cutting the grass. He was appreciative, and before continuing on with his work he told me the new owner was in the office if I wanted to talk to her. I returned to my car and drove up to the office, again with only the intention of saying thank you. And again, after introducing myself and explaining why I was there, and of the stress I had endured, I thanked her. Just like the young man cutting grass, she was appreciative, but she also added that if I signed a waiver I was more than welcome to dig up the urn myself. I didn't need a permit. I didn't have to pay any money. I could just bring a shovel and do what I had to do. That wasn't the reason for my unplanned visit to the cemetery that day, but I was ecstatic when I left. Time for a new plan.

My head was spinning with this new knowledge, and then it hit me like a ton of bricks. That magical place in the magical forest, that was it!! I knew it was special the second I came upon it with the sun struggling to shine through the tall trees and the sound of the creek trickling by. This is where I wanted Dani's ashes. This is exactly where she was supposed to be.

I could have waited until the weekend so my husband would have been able to help me, but I didn't want to wait. I wanted it done, and I wanted it done now. After providing the owner of the cemetery a copy of my Power of Attorney document, and then signing the waiver, I got to work. I knew exactly where Dani's urn was, directly under her headstone. After digging up the headstone, which was not easy as it weighed well over 100 pounds, I was able to start digging where I knew the urn containing her ashes to be. I got down to my knees and started digging with my hands. I didn't want to hit the marble urn with the full-size shovel, and regrettably, I didn't bring anything smaller, so I dug using only my hands. I probably looked like a crazy person to all who drove by. The entire cemetery, and Dani's grave, was perfectly visible to the busy, high traffic road that ran alongside the cemetery, and choosing to do this in the middle of the day, a weekday, traffic was at its peak. Dani's grave was situated right on top of the hill, probably the most visible area of the entire

cemetery, and I'm on my hands
and knees frantically digging in
a grave like a dog. I'm sure I
was quite a sight!

After locating Dani's
urn, I carefully wrapped it in a
blanket and placed it in my car.
I brought an extra blanket with
the intention of placing the
headstone on the blanket in
order to drag it to my car. I
knew I could get it in my trunk
once there, I just didn't want
to try to carry that 100+ pound
headstone across the cemetery.
I could get it, I would get it,
but the nice young man that was
cutting the grass that day,
knowing exactly what I was
doing, came over to offer
assistance. He loaded the
headstone and a cement bench
that was also at her grave, onto
a four-wheeler and took them to
my car. He even placed them in
my trunk. I was so grateful for
the entire experience. I was
grateful to the new owner
allowing me to do what I had
been trying to do for years. I

was grateful to the kind young man that was cutting the grass that day which initiated my impromptu visit. Technically, I still owned Dani's grave even though I removed everything. I could have tried to sell it, or whatever, but to show my gratitude I donated the plot back to the cemetery, even though it was only $75. I never wanted to set foot in that cemetery again!

I was done with that cemetery, but I also never wanted to see the headstone again. My brother, my offender, after placing his arm around my shoulder during Dani's viewing ten years prior, asked me the question, "Was this my fault?" How do you respond to that, especially in that environment, standing over the corpse of your dead sister? My brother, my offender, The Invisible Monster, purchased that headstone that was covering Dani's ashes for the past ten years. I dragged the heavy headstone across my father's new, very large backyard until I reached the edge of the forest. I wanted the headstone gone, but I didn't feel right about throwing it away or destroying it. I wrapped it in the same blanket I used to drag it across the yard and buried it in the edge of the forest. It was gone.

Making multiple trips from my car to the magical spot in the forest, I managed to get the urn containing Dani's ashes, the cement bench from the cemetery, the wrought iron trellis I previously purchased intending to put at the cemetery, my shovel, and whatever other supplies I thought I might need to create my new masterpiece. I found large rocks in the nearby creek bed and created a small circle in the center of that magical spot, kind of like you would create for a campfire. After strategically placing the trellis in the area with the most sunshine and placing the cement bench near the newly formed rock circle, I was ready. In anticipation of my next task, I brought a hammer and a small flathead screwdriver. The urn was a small marble box and the only way to access the contents was pry the tightly secured bottom piece open with the hammer and screwdriver. The urn had been buried underground for the past ten years, exposed to groundwater from rain and snow. It had been frozen in the winter; it had been heated in the summer. And rather than wearing it down, all that exposure seemed to tighten the seal. My only option was to bust through the bottom piece, cracking through the marble to create a hole large enough to remove its contents, Dani's ashes.

I didn't really know what to expect. I had never seen cremated human remains before. It was mostly ashes, but there were still unburned bone fragments throughout. I laid Dani's ashes in the middle of the rock circle I created. As I was smoothing the small mound with my bare hand, feeling the ashes and bones that were once my baby sister, I surprised myself with the words that came out of my mouth. "You are so beautiful!" Where did that come from? There was no thought whatsoever. I just opened my mouth, and those words came out. But you know what? It was beautiful. She had been trapped in that box, the small marble urn buried in the ground at that horrible pet cemetery, for the past ten years. I felt like I was trapped in that box right along with her. "You are so beautiful!" The act of letting her ashes go back to nature was beautiful. We were both free.

46 ~ Rewind – That Guy That Caught My Eye

"We never wanted to give up at the same time."

~ Grandma

My grandmother was a wise woman. When asked the secret to having a loving, long-term marriage she would reply, "We never wanted to give up at the same time." This is one of the truest statements I have ever heard. I have been doing life with that guy that caught my eye for 24 years, married 18, and I love him more today than I ever have. It's been a wild ride, like a roller coaster with all its ups and downs, but like my wise grandmother said, "We never wanted to give up at the same time."

47 ~ Panhandle

Although I didn't make the decision to move in with my boyfriend three weeks after we started dating, which changed the course for my entire life, I know now that it was supposed to happen that way. I honestly believe that we were meant to be together. If we hadn't lived together, I may have tried to push him away like I did everyone else. If we hadn't lived together, I may not have been able to have Dani. I could say that about a lot of things, "if we hadn't lived together." As I said, it was meant to be.

Late in 1999, Dani went to Ohio to live with Ashely for a short time. This was after her first suicide attempt with Tylenol. Her father was out of prison for the second time, and after finding her in West Virginia with me, and knowing of a suicide attempt, he decided to bring her back to Ohio. I had obviously failed with her, so I agreed. Even at 14 Dani was a lot to handle, and I honestly thought living with Ashely would help. I'm not exactly sure why she was going to live with Ashely and not her father, but whatever. I really thought Ashely would be able to help her, but after a few months she dropped her off at my mother's house.

Obviously, I didn't handle her leaving well. Not only had I failed with her, but I also really missed her too. And now she was back with our mother and her abusive boyfriend. Yeah, I wasn't handling it well at all. The depression I went into caused some rocky months for sure, my boyfriend and I even separated for four months. But the universe had bigger plans, we were meant to be together. The separation didn't last long.

With Dani in Ohio, we had a lot more freedom, so we were

quick to accept temporary jobs
in Texas. Our friend, the same
friend that lived with my
boyfriend when I moved in, the
same friend that was spinning
the Siamese cat like a propeller
on my first visit to the Animal
Kingdom, was now a traveling
electrician. He was in Texas on
a job, and they needed a lot of
help, so we went. I recently
graduated from college and we
were completely free. We packed
up the car, picked up another
friend, and drove to Texas.

We stayed in a boarding
house for three weeks in a small
town called Panhandle, Texas,
which is just as you would
imagine located in the panhandle
of Texas. The house was really
old but clean enough. My
boyfriend and I had a bedroom
and a small kitchen, but the
only bathroom was a common
bathroom in the hallway. The
town of Panhandle was really old
and really small. The few
small, one-story buildings were
the typical old-style, clay

buildings like you see in the movies. It was an interesting experience, to say the least.

The work was even more interesting. I had never done electrical work before as a profession, but growing up with a carpenter father, and a mother with a "can-do" attitude, I was fully capable to do any task required of me. Honestly, I was probably more capable than my boyfriend. Of course, he was capable, I just had way more experience. The location of the job was a little unsettling, but the job paid extremely well so I gave it a shot. We were working on a new addition to an existing, functioning beef packing plant in the middle of the desert. I wasn't a vegetarian or anything, although I had toyed with it in the past. I ate hamburgers and steak, Arby's roast beef sandwiches, etc. I ate meat, so again, I gave it a shot. Me being a small person, with small hands, I was placed on the roof of the newly built structure. With my small hands, the delicate wirework connecting each of the mechanical systems that were placed on that new roof was perfect for me. Being on the roof in the middle of the desert also gave me a perfect view in all directions, and off in the distance, the view was beautiful and massive.

The problem, however, was the up close and personal view of every single semi-truck with trailer after trailer of cows on their way to be slaughtered. I was close enough to hear the horrible sounds of fear coming from the cows crammed in those trailers all day long. They made all kinds of noises, definitely not contained to "mooing" alone. Just as I had a perfect view of the probable 100s of full cow trucks going in, I had the same perfect view of the empty cow trucks going out. It was a little overwhelming. It didn't help that I heard a nonchalant description of the slaughtering process for each of those scared cows on those trucks by a fellow electrician.

The first part of the process is a nail to the skull by an industrial-sized nail gun designed specifically for this purpose, killing the cow instantly, except when it doesn't. For the second part of the process, the cow is then hung up on a meat hook and skinned. If the initial nail to the skull fails to kill the cow, which happens more than I care to think about, the live cow, already scared from transport, and now in pain from having a nail driven into its brain, is then strung up alive so its skin can be painfully ripped from its body. Full cow trucks going in, empty cow trucks going out. It was more than I could handle, money or not. I became a vegetarian for a while and spent the rest of our time in Panhandle in our boarding house alone, or wandering the small,

dilapidated town while my
boyfriend continued to work.
The cow trucks didn't affect him
quite like they did me, but then
again, he didn't have the same
rooftop view that I had.

I made the best of my time.
I read, I worked out, I prepared
meals, I explored the small
town, I kept busy. We explored
even further during my
boyfriend's time off. After a
phone call to his mother to
check in, my boyfriend told me
that Dani had tried to call. My
mother didn't have a phone, and
Dani was living with her, so the
only way I could reach her was
to call her at school. Again,
this was before cell phones were
so prevalent. But once I was
able to reach her, I decided
then and there I was going to
bring her back to West Virginia
once we returned. For one
thing, she wanted to come back.
The only reason I was okay with
her leaving in the first place
was that she was going to live
with Ashely. Before leaving for

Texas I sent Dani money to buy a winter coat, which my mother had taken and spent while promising to buy her one later. My mother had used that excuse on me so many times in the past that I knew the money was gone for good. I had to get her back as soon as possible, but in the meantime, it was cold in Ohio and Dani didn't have a coat. This is also when my mother's abusive boyfriend broke her arm, right in front of Dani, by pushing her down a flight of stairs. I was more upset that Dani was in that environment than the fact that my mother had been hurt, and I could not wait to get back.

48 ~ Galveston

With me no longer working, and now anxious to get back to Dani, we decided to cut our work trip short. After three weeks we were on our way home, but rather than driving straight through we decided to take the scenic route. With pockets full of money, our trunk loaded up, and our friends in the back seat, we drove south. We drove through Houston, and then onto Galveston, Texas, which is a small island city on the Gulf Coast of Texas. To get to Galveston you have to take a short trip on a ferry. Even that short ferry ride proved to be an adventure.

Through this time, I never stopped smoking weed. I didn't drink alcohol. Other than experimenting with acid as a teenager, and then a brief stint with Ecstasy (now, that's a fun one), weed stayed my drug of choice. Although I brought a small amount of weed with me for the trip it had been depleted long before we started our return trip. And then I spotted something, a Zig-Zag sticker on the back window of the car directly in front of us. It wasn't an obvious Zig-Zag sticker, but one that would only be recognized by a fellow pothead. Really wanting weed for our road trip, and listening to my intuition, I knew I would be able to get it from the person in that car, on a ferry on the Gulf of Mexico. I couldn't even see the person in the car ahead, but with my intuition screaming loud and clear I got out of the car and walked up to the driver's side window. The driver was a young woman, probably close to my age, and had a hippish appearance. I introduced myself and explained my reason for approaching her. She was very nice and understanding and offered to meet us later. I told her we were just passing through and

wouldn't be around later. That
very nice and understanding
"hippie" on the ferry reached
over to her glove compartment
and pulled out a large bag of
weed. She placed that large bag
of weed in my hand. I tried to
pay her, but she called it a
gift. I walked back to my car
with a smile on my face and we
were on our way.

We made it to our beach
destination in Galveston just as
it was getting dark. All four
of us got out of the car and
walked through the sand to the
edge of the Gulf of Mexico. I
didn't know at the time but
driving to the beach in
Galveston was all part of a
bigger plan. Once we got to the
edge of the water my boyfriend
grabbed my hand and guided me
off to the right, our friends
immediately went to the left.
Once alone my boyfriend stopped
to face me with a smile on his
face, pulled a ring out of his
pocket, and got down on one
knee. With that same smile on

his face, he held out a beautiful, and completely unexpected, diamond ring and asked me to marry him. We had already lived together for the majority of our four-year relationship by this time, so of course, this was the next logical step. But I was still caught off guard by the location and timing of his proposal. It was beautiful! It was romantic! It was perfect! I said yes without hesitation, and I too had a smile on my face.

We continued on our scenic route all along the southern coastline. We made a pit stop in New Orleans and spent the evening on Bourbon Street. This was before the town was demolished from Hurricane Katrina in 2005. It was such a neat, and wild place with such a deeply rooted history. I'm happy we were able to experience it before the hurricane.

We eventually made it back to West Virginia after one more

pit stop in Tennessee, although
this stop wasn't planned. Right
outside a large city, maybe
Knoxville, while driving along
the interstate in the middle of
the night, one of the car tires
blew out. A flat tire is always
inconvenient, but it's even more
inconvenient when it happens on
the interstate in the middle of
the night in Tennessee. And
even more inconvenient with a
trunk packed to the rim of the
belongings of four people that
had been traveling for a month,
tools, clothes, a couple sets of
dumbbells, souvenirs, etc. In
the middle of the night, on the
side of the interstate, we
carefully unpacked the entire
contents of the trunk placing
our belongings on the side of
the road, only to find the jack
was missing. We borrowed my
boyfriend's mother's car for the
trip to Texas and it never
occurred to me to check the
spare tire and jack before we
left. Well, crap…

49 ~ Arzona Acres

Finally, back in West Virginia, living in The Animal Kingdom with my fiancé, I was able to make arrangements for Dani to come back. Since Dani was living with my mother at the time the process was easy. My mother didn't protest at all. And once back in West Virginia Dani did extremely well. She was doing well in school. She wasn't abusing prescription pills or anything else for that matter. She was working on getting her 15-year-old work permit so she could get a job. She had a nice boyfriend. I kind of think she was scared of being sent back to Ohio and was trying to be on her best behavior, but she seemed happy. I was happy too.

Dani's boyfriend was nice, but their relationship didn't last. After an argument about her going to a party without

him, he broke up with her.
Honestly, I think he was just
looking for a reason to break up
with her. After he broke up
with her he started dating my
best friend, Rhett. So yeah,
their relationship never would
have worked out, him being gay
and all. But two weeks after
they broke up Dani found out she
was pregnant. She was 15 and
alone. When she told him he was
obviously upset but didn't have
much to say about it. Dani made
the decision to have an
abortion, and I supported her
decision. What did I know? I
had never been pregnant. I had
never been in the position to
have to decide something like
that.

One of my biggest regrets
in life is not handling that
situation differently. That
decision to abort her baby
haunted Dani until the day she
died. I feel that having that
abortion came as a great
consequence to her. If I would
have known I could have tried to

369

convince her to keep the baby,
or I could have offered to keep
the baby for myself to raise.
Or going back a little further,
I could have taken her to be put
on birth control. I didn't do
any of that, I just supported
her decision. I was 21 raising
a 15-year-old, what the Hell did
I know? For the next four
years, I watched her suffer from
that decision, always saying the
say the same thing, "I killed my
baby."

Life went on, I got a job
with a local foster care agency
called Braley & Thompson. My
fiancé decided not to go to
college after receiving his GED,
so he was already working full-
time. We were engaged, we were
both working, it was time to
start our adult life. We saved
up some cash and got the heck
out of The Animal Kingdom.

50 ~ Stuart Acres

Our first apartment was in a small sub-division in Kolasi, West Virginia called Stuart Acres. It was a small, two-bedroom apartment, one room for us, one room for Dani. Our apartment was nice, and it was very clean, unlike The Animal Kingdom. We had nice things and nice neighbors. Dani was able to attend the same school and could catch the bus at the end of the street. Life was good!

Shortly after we moved into our apartment, after seeing Dani off to school, I arrived at work ready for the day. I was working as a file clerk for Braley & Thompson and spent my days alone in the file room, just me and a radio. The first thing I did every morning when I got to work was turn on the radio, and this morning was no exception. At first, I thought it was a joke, but I quickly realized something was wrong. The date was September 11, 2001, and the first of the Twin Towers had just been struck by an airplane. While listening to the radio, and still trying to comprehend what I had just heard, it was announced that the second building had been struck. The whole country went into an instant panic, me included. Dani called me from school, also scared, and asked me to pick her up, which I did. The multiple terrorist attacks changed our country forever that day.

Dani lived with us for most of the time we lived in that apartment, but near the end, she decided to go back to The Animal Kingdom. Dani was really close with my fiancé's sister, who was around the same age as her, and she wanted to live with her. Letting her go is another one of my big regrets. The responsibility of taking care of Dani was a lot, emotionally and financially. It was time-consuming and exhausting. I think she knew it was wearing me down, which is probably one of the reasons she wanted to go. I think she also wanted more freedom. Without me constantly looking over her shoulder, freedom is exactly what she had. "Xani-Dani" was formed.

My fiancé and I had freedom too. This was the first time in our entire relationship we had ever lived alone. We had been together five years, we were engaged, I was 23, he was 21. It was time for the next step in our life. We weren't actually thinking of having a baby yet, but after a devastating comment by a doctor saying that I probably wouldn't be able to get pregnant. He said even if I were to get pregnant, I probably wouldn't be able to carry a baby. We decided to give it a shot. I have that same "can-do" attitude that my mother has, and I don't like to be told I can't do something. That doctor said I couldn't get pregnant, and I had to prove him wrong, which I

did almost instantly. The very
first month I was off birth
control I got pregnant. Of
course, I was excited, but the
look on my fiancé's face and the
single tear of joy that escaped
his left eye made it clear we
made the right decision. We
were going to have a baby!

51 ~ Clayton Valley

Shortly after my fiancé and I found out we were going to have a baby we moved to a three-bedroom house, which we ended up staying in for quite some time. Even to this day, it's probably the longest I have ever stayed in one place. It was a very basic ranch-style house right on Clayton Valley Road. The house was literally brown from top to bottom. The outside had tan siding. The inside was brown carpet and brown wood paneling as far as the eye could see, but we loved it anyway. We had a nice backyard if you could tune out the busy road. Our only neighbors were the maids from the cleaning service next door. Clayton Valley Road was a very busy two-lane road when we moved in, but shortly after we moved in they started the two-year process of widening the road.

We spent time planning a wedding long before we were going to have a baby, but nothing ever stuck. There were a lot of reasons for this, but ultimately, I think it was because I was scared. Other than my grandparents, every single person I knew who got married also got divorced. I didn't want to get married only to get divorced later. Another obstacle was money, we didn't have any. Neither one of us came from the type of family that would help with anything like that. If we wanted a wedding, we would be paying for it ourselves. All wedding planning was halted though when my father mentioned walking me down the aisle. He wanted to walk me down the aisle, and then "give me away." Give me away? Hadn't he already done that? He "gave me away" when he told me I wasn't allowed to come home that day. He "gave me away" when he sabotaged my high school education. He "gave me away" when he didn't protect me from

The Invisible Monster. He "gave
me away" a long time ago and I
wasn't going to let him do it
again.

Six years after we started
dating, after being engaged for
two years, and seven months
pregnant, we went to the
courthouse and got married.
Guiltily, my main motivation to
finally getting married was
because I wanted to have the
same last name as my baby. Of
course, I loved my fiancé and I
wanted to be married to him, but
I didn't want to wait any
longer. Our baby was going to
be born soon. We decided to go
on October 18th, 2002, which was
Dani's birthday. We really
liked the idea at first. We
weren't trying to take away her
special day, it was more in
honor of her. I think she liked
the idea too. We stopped
celebrating our anniversary
after she died. October 18th,
2005 would have been her 20th
birthday, our third anniversary.

Our son was born on December 31st, 2002. That doctor that said I probably couldn't get pregnant was very wrong. I was closely monitored with weekly doctor visits throughout my entire pregnancy, which ended in a c-section and a giant 8-pound, 15-ounce, 22 inches healthy, baby boy. I didn't realize how extremely large he was until much later. They said he was big, but he looked so small to me. It wasn't until people around me started having babies that I realized he actually was quite large.

I was in love, a love so deep I didn't know was possible. I loved that baby boy more than life itself. But with that love, I became angry, extremely angry. I wasn't angry about having a baby. I was so happy to be a mother. Looking at my beautiful baby, and knowing how much I loved him, I became angry with my mother. I became angry with my father. I became angry

with Dani's father. Basically,
I became angry at all the adults
that had let me and my sisters
down. It never made much sense
to me, but now, knowing how what
it felt like to have a child, it
really didn't make sense. How
could a mother not love and
protect her baby? I really did
learn a lot about being a good
mother from my mother though.
By my mother's example, I
learned what not to do.

I became angry, but I also
became scared. The Invisible
Monster, although in hiding, was
never far from my mind; that
damn Invisible Monster and all
those unanswered questions.
After my brother graduated from
high school he joined the
military, so he had been gone
for a while. I rarely had to
see him, but now that I had a
baby to protect. I wanted
nothing to do with him. My
father was around, but it was
complicated. I didn't trust him
with my baby either. All those
unanswered questions were all-

consuming. I say it's complicated because my father is the only grandparent that has ever truly wanted to be involved, and he has been an amazing grandfather, but The Invisible Monster came from somewhere.

Symptoms of The Invisible Monster were not contained to my untrusting nature. I now realized how vulnerable we are when we sleep. I never really made the connection before, but Dani slept in my arms for the first half of her life. I know now I was protecting her from The Invisible Monster that visited me far too often in my sleep. Knowing how vulnerable we are when we sleep and knowing I had to protect my baby from all the evils of the world, of course, he slept in my arms. I was breastfeeding, and it really did make things easier, having him sleep in my arms, but it was more than that. I HAD to sleep with him in my arms. I HAD to feel him breathing. I HAD to

hear every sound he made. I HAD
to know that he was safe.
Although I only breastfed him
for 14 months, I slept with him
in my arms until he was five.

        Shortly after our baby was
born Dani came to live with us
after an unpleasant incident at
The Animal Kingdom. She called
in the middle of the night
asking to be picked up because
she woke up to some random guy
in her room trying to have sex
with her. She had no idea who
he was, just that he was a guest
of my husband's sister. The
unpleasant incident resulted in
my husband going back to The
Animal Kingdom the next morning,
pulling another random guy out
of his sister's bed, beating his
ass. It wasn't the same guy
that was in Dani's room the
previous night, but it didn't
matter. He just said, "Pass
this message on to your
friends," during the beatdown.
We loved having Dani back, not
that she was ever really gone.
Even when she was living in The

Animal Kingdom for those few months, we were still together all the time. But having her back, living under our roof felt good. I wish she would have stayed with us forever.

We had our second son on July 23rd, 2008. This pregnancy was a difficult one, with multiple hospital stays, eight to be exact. But on that eighth stay our son was born by c-section. He was three weeks early and he wasn't breathing when he came out. Of course, no one told me he wasn't breathing. My abdomen was open and if I started freaking it could have gone really bad. I couldn't see where they took my baby, but I could see my husband standing near him. I was so happy, and it was obvious by the big smile on my face as I was looking at my husband. He was looking at me, smiling at him, and looking at our baby who wasn't breathing. I can't imagine the turmoil he was experiencing, watching his baby unable to breathe, knowing he couldn't tell me, or I may bleed out. Once they got him breathing they brought him over to me and I saw his sweet, beautiful face. I knew my family was complete.

Even though our second baby was three weeks early he was still quite large, 7-pounds, 14-ounces, and 21-inches. Although I wish he would have stayed in a little longer if he had he probably would have weighed ten pounds. His lungs could have used a little more time, and he hadn't gained his fat yet since that's typically what happens the last few weeks of pregnancy, but he was okay. I was a different story; my body was trashed. I am a very small person who grew giant babies, and my body couldn't recover, which ultimately led to a hysterectomy 18 months after his birth.

52 ~ Unblocked

I love my hysterectomy and I feel that it was necessary for my healing. Obviously, it healed my physical problems, but it was more than that. Once my physical problems were addressed I realized I still had a huge mental block to overcome, which was deeply ingrained. I can't say that I didn't enjoy having sex with my husband, I did, but I honestly thought that orgasms were something made up, and only men had them. Boy was I wrong! One thing about my husband is that he is very goal-oriented, and lucky for me his goal was to teach me how to have an orgasm. My brain was so damaged from The Invisible Monster that I developed an "off switch," but he was determined. And oddly, learning how to flip my switch from off to on scared the crap out of me. The second I would start to feel that new sensation I would panic and push him away,

and then he would "push" harder.
Oh, my goodness, I am so
grateful he did! I was 32 when
I had my first orgasm, and let
me tell you, my husband awakened
a sleeping beast. For the first
time in my life, I loved sex! I
craved sex with my husband. I
honestly didn't think it was
possible to feel the things I
was feeling, it's like I finally
understood how it was supposed
to be. I was unblocked.

53 ~ Money Sucks

I could go through all our
financial stresses, but what's
the point. I could talk about
fighting shutoff notices. I
could talk about borrowing money
just so we could have food. I
could talk about the time my
husband got laid off on the same
day we closed on our house. I
have always hated money, or at
least the power it has over us.
I don't like that money can
dictate our happiness, but
unfortunately, it does. My
husband worked his ass off,
sometimes working three jobs at
a time. So, if I were to place
blame on someone for our
financial stress it would have
to be placed on me. I could not
leave my boys. I could not put
them in daycare or have a
babysitter. I typically worked
from home, or part-time opposite
my husband's schedule, which
limited our time together, but
at least I knew our boys were

safe. The few times I tried a
regular, full-time job I would
end up quitting after a few
months. If I wasn't 100%
available for my boys my anxiety
would be through the roof. I
understand the psychology behind
this, but it sure didn't help
our financial situation. As
stressful as it was though I am
blessed to have an understanding
husband. He never blamed me.
He wanted me home with the boys
too, and he understood exactly
why I had trouble leaving them.
He just worked twice as hard,
and I am so grateful.

My husband became a police
officer in 2010. To become a
police officer in the state of
West Virginia is a little
different than most states. To
become a police officer in West
Virginia you must first be
chosen by a department, and then
that department will send you to
the West Virginia State Police
Academy. It is a live-in
academy, like the most extreme
boot camp you can imagine. The
Marines that were in the academy
with my husband said that the
police academy was way more
difficult. The only bonus was
they were allowed to go home on
the weekends.

Our oldest son was seven
and our younger son turned two
shortly after my husband went
into the police academy. He
lived there for almost five
months, which was hard enough,

but the academy was literally two miles away from our house. The West Virginia State Police Academy sits on top of a hill alongside the interstate, so almost every time we left our house we passed it. He was so close, yet we couldn't see him. Every single time we passed I honked the horn and didn't let up until the academy was out of sight just in case, he was outside. I'm sure being so close to the interstate he heard a lot of horns, but I like to think he heard my horn, too, even if he didn't know it was mine.

I was so proud of my husband, he was an incredible police officer, but our family life was suffering. I referred to myself as being "married/single" during that time. I was married, and we did have him in spurts, but 95% of the time it was just me and the boys. My husband worked swing shift, as well as 12+ hour shifts, but just because he got

to that 12-hour mark did not
mean he came home right then.
The thing about bad guys is
they're not on a timeclock, they
don't care if it's almost time
for shift change. I can't even
list all the holidays, school
events, sporting and Ju Jitsu
events, and vacations we had to
do without him. Our youngest
son even spent five days in the
hospital with tubes in all of
his orifices while his father
was in the police academy and
unable to leave. Many
Christmases were celebrated at
4:00 a.m. just so we could
celebrate together before he
left for work.

For a short time, we lived
in the city where my husband was
a police officer, which had its
perks. The downfalls definitely
outweighed the perks. There
were many occasions when the
boys and I would be walking to
the library, or wherever, and we
would see him out "dealing" with
someone. I would have to tell
the boys, "Act like you don't

know Daddy," because my husband did not want anyone to know who his family was. He feared we could become potential targets. He didn't even want me to have an F.O.P. (Fraternal Order of Police) sticker on my car even though we were members. It was hard knowing all of our neighbors' secrets, too. Maybe I would make a comment to my husband about not seeing one of the kids at school all week and he would reply, "Oh, that's because I arrested her mom on Saturday." We had been attending a church in the city, but people at church have secrets, too, and even that started causing problems. Our family became a deterrent for potential churchgoers. We didn't want to stand in anyone's way of going to church, so we left.

At times his job was too much to handle. The day before school started one year I was at the police gym with the boys while my husband was working.

While we were there he called to see if we were home yet. I told him we were not. He instantly said, "Go home right now. Lock the doors and close the curtains. We are getting ready to serve a no-knock warrant across the street from our house and there are supposed to be a lot of guns in there." We left instantly, no questions asked. The police station and police gym were only three blocks from our house, so we made it home and safely inside with the doors locked pretty quickly. With all the blinds and curtains closed, I took the boys to the back of the house, the furthest point from the soon-to-be-searched house across the street. Once I had the boys settled, I returned to the front. I peeked out the front window and my heart sank. I saw multiple police cars parked in the front yard right across from our house, all awkward, with the lights flashing. The front door had been shattered with a battering ram. I didn't see any police

officers anywhere. I knew they
were inside the house with a guy
who was said to be dangerous,
and supposedly had a lot of
guns. And my husband was
inside. I watched and waited as
the neighbors were starting to
gather outside, one even knocked
on my door to see what was going
on. That actually kind of
pissed me off and my reply was,
"I'm trying not to puke, that's
what's going on," then slammed
the door. They took the guy out
the back door and everything was
ultimately fine, but I didn't
know that. I was scared to
death for my husband while I
patiently waited to hear from
him.

We eventually moved out of
the city and things definitely
improved, but I still found
myself using the phrase,
"Glorious life of an officer's
wife," quite often. I was
always supportive and proud, and
we made it work, but it wasn't
the life we wanted. It was
crushing for my husband that his

family's life was passing him by. His boys were growing up and he was missing it. And they were missing him, I was missing him. And that's not even mentioning my fear. Every day my husband walked out the front door to go to work I knew there was a chance I would never see him again. I can't even count the times he called and said he was going to be late because he was getting stitches, or he was involved in a crash, or bitten by a dog. There was even a human bite once which required a tetanus shot and bloodwork. He has been involved in a shooting where the suspect lost his life. On so many occasions he would leave his boots by the door and tell me not to touch them because they were covered in blood. I have had to bring him clean uniforms in the middle of the night because the stench of a decaying human tends to cling quite nicely to polyester uniforms. My husband has never once walked out the door in our 24-year relationship without saying, "I love you," but it was even more important during his career as a police officer.

The last Christmas he spent as a police officer consisted of me holding back my tears all day while trying to make sure the boys were having a good day. We did our usual 4:00 a.m. Christmas at home before he left for work that morning. My husband's grandparents lived in the same city he worked, so the boys and I drove up there with plans of him stopping by while on duty. I called him once we arrived at his grandparents' house and he was there within a few minutes. But once he got out of the car I knew something was wrong. He walked up to the door and said he just got a call, that he couldn't stay. He briefly greeted his grandparents and the boys, kissed me, then walked back to his car. That day, at that particular moment, it was more than I could handle. I hated his job! I hated our life! Yet, I stayed the

supportive wife, and never once
asked him to give it up.
Glorious life of an officer's
wife…

55 ~ Nah...Bigger

I always knew there was something special about my husband, even way back when I made the remark, "He'll be cute when he gets older." Through all our trials and tribulation, our trauma, our financial stress, his constant love and support of me and my crazy brain, he never faltered. I must say, my husband was an amazing police officer. He always caught the bad guys. I'm talking about the truly bad guys. He never cared much for silly traffic tickets or even simple possession of marijuana. He wanted the child molesters and rapists, he wanted the murderers, he wanted the wife beaters, and he was damn good at his job. But look at the cost, his family was suffering. His life was passing by and he was missing it.

Our life was about to change in the most unexpected way. When I say there is something special about my husband, I mean it, and not like a typical wife's opinion of her husband kind of thing. There is seriously something special about him. While all the other police officers were sitting in their cruisers playing games or watching movies on their phones, or taking naps at the station, or all kinds of other things that I will keep to myself, my husband was reading Napoleon Hill's old writings or studying The Law of Attraction. He became rather obsessed with reading, and studying, and learning anything that could potentially make our lives better. I will admit, I didn't understand what was happening in the beginning, but my husband was changing and in a very good way. Without this change I know we wouldn't be where we are today, and today life is pretty damn good.

My husband applied for a
job he wasn't technically
qualified for, but with his
experience as a police officer
and his new way of thinking he
applied anyway. The
qualification he was missing was
a top-secret security clearance.
He did work part-time with the
U.S. Marshalls, so he had a
lower-level clearance. I'm sure
that helped some, but I feel it
was The Law of Attraction at
play. He was offered a job.
They even paid for his top-
secret clearance, which actually
was quite an ordeal and took
over a year to complete. But
once it was complete our life
took off. The job was still in
West Virginia, but a couple
hours from where we were
currently living. When his
start date came in the boys
still had four months left of
school. We hadn't sold our
house. We hadn't found a new
house. We were nowhere near
ready to leave.

Yes, the Law of Attraction came into play in getting the job, but now was the time we really needed it. The idea of the Law of Attraction is basically picturing what you want, whether it be a job, a car, a way of life, it doesn't matter, and picturing it as though you already have it. We were getting ready to make some major sacrifices to achieve the life we wanted. I am so thankful that we did, but it was rough. My husband lived in a hotel for those four months, only coming home on weekends while the boys finished out the school year. It was expensive and we were poor. Yes, this new job paid better, but hotels are expensive, and we dug a pretty deep financial hole. But as we were digging that hole, we were also picturing ourselves climbing right back out. I knew we were working towards something good. I never in a million years expected how good.

My husband's new job was just a stepping-stone. Shortly after we all got up there he applied for another job with an even higher clearance level required, along with a master's degree. My husband with his confidence and motivation applied anyway, with his GED and inadequate clearance level. They offered him a job! The government signed a waiver allowing him to work there even though he didn't have the required master's degree. This was only the second time in the history of the company that had been done. He had a financial goal of reaching six figures by age 45, he made it at 39. Although money is nice, really nice, I don't want to focus on that. I knew were going to be better financially once things were settled.

56 ~ Life Gets Interesting

Our boys were 14 and eight when we relocated, they are now 18 and 12. We moved fairly often so the boys were used to starting over, but unbeknownst to us, this move would change the course of our lives forever. We were always big on keeping our boys in extra-curricular activities. With our older son, those activities usually consisted of Ju Jitsu, MMA, wrestling, guitar lessons, etc. Our younger son was different though. From a very young age he decided he wanted to be an actor. He tried Ju-Jitsu, Lego League (engineering club), and a few other things, but his heart was set on acting. I wanted to help him pursue his passion, but I had no idea how to even start with something like acting.

The town we relocated to is actually a college town. For a field trip, our son went to the play, To Kill a Mockingbird, that the college theatre program was performing. The cast were all college students except one little girl, a little girl that was in our son's third-grade class. That was incredible news to me! I knew what I had to do to make my son's dreams come true. Occasionally, I would sit in and help with Lego League, which was an after-school program. I knew that same little girl was in Lego League, too, so I had him point her out to me. I had a plan; I was going to talk to her mother after Lego League to find out how we could pursue acting. Her dad actually picked her up, but he relayed the message and I spoke with her mother later that evening. She told me about a children's theater and arts program through the local college and gave me the contact information. He started acting classes right away.

This theater program has a large children's production

every year, in which you need to audition and be cast. Just because you're enrolled in classes does not mean you are guaranteed a part. He auditioned with all the confidence in the world, for a fairly large role, which would entail singing multiple solos and a lot of dancing, neither of which he had any experience in. He didn't care, he knew what he wanted, and he went for it. He didn't get that specific part but was still cast in a significant role. And so, it begins.

Knowing that our son had an interest in acting a friend passed on a casting call that she came across on social media. The casting call was for a film being made in our area by a local filmmaker. After looking into I realized that he was too young to audition and I never mentioned it to him. I will admit, something like that would have stopped me in the past. I was starting to look at life differently though. I requested information along with a heartfelt email introducing our son and his passion for acting. I asked for him to be considered anyway, even though he was too young. The most he could do is say no, but he didn't say no. Our son was invited to audition…and was cast in his first film, and then a second, and a third. He's up to seven films and is now a professional commercial actor as well. Acting and modeling go hand in hand; he is also a nationally recognized model and a local runway model.

In the beginning, I found myself saying quite often, "He's the actor, we're just along for the ride." He was moving forward full steam ahead and taking us right along with him. I was very involved in every film project he was in, either as an extra or just behind the scenes help. Our older son was also recruited as a model while tagging along as the supportive big brother; they now are both runway models and do fashion shows together. Through all of these film and modeling endeavors, we have met some amazing people, and with these amazing people, we have been inspired. My husband and I are both published authors. We're models and have been featured in multiple magazines and social media platforms. We have been guests on podcasts, as a family of four and as a couple. My husband is the owner of a fitness/nutrition company. We are even in the process of starting our own podcast. And every day more opportunities are presenting themselves. If someone would have told me, even three years ago, we would be where we are, and doing the things we are doing, I would have laughed and thought they were crazy. But here we are! Isn't life interesting?

57 ~ Life is Pretty Damn Good

It has taken me a long time to have to confidence to tell my story. My story is not a story of hate. My story is not a story of trauma. I'm not telling my story to be vindictive. I don't even hold a grudge. I was once told, "Holding a grudge is like having a noose around your neck, it only hurts you." I have forgiven my Monsters for my own peace of mind. My story is a story of HOPE. My story is a story of INSPIRATION. I'm telling my story to encourage others to shoot for the stars no matter what their reality is. From a two-year-old forest kid who was forced to perform oral sex on her brother to a wife (with an amazing sex life I might add), mother, published author, model, actor, podcast host, and I'm just getting started. We all have the power to create the life we want, and

I am living proof. I'm not only
surviving, I'm thriving! And
life is pretty damn good…

"You can't go back and change
the beginning, but you can start
where you are and change the
ending."

~ James Sherman

*In loving memory of my baby sister, Dani
(Danielle Renee 10/18/85-9/9/05). I pray that
you have found your peace, although I'd rather
you be here with me.*